MORE THINGS TO DO IN CHILDREN'S WORSHIP

BY SUSAN SAYERS

Kevin Mayhew

First published in 1996 by
KEVIN MAYHEW LTD
Rattlesden
Bury St Edmunds
Suffolk IP30 0SZ

More Things to Do in Children's Worship is adapted
from *Springboard Two* by Susan Sayers,
published by Kevin Mayhew Ltd, 1994.

ISBN 0 86209 793 2
Catalogue No 1500043

Cover illustrated by Sarah Silcock

Editor: Michael Forster
Typesetting by Louise Hill
Printed and bound in Great Britain.

Foreword

In this book, I hope to provide material for use in children's worship which is helpful to those churches which do not follow a set programme of readings and themes. The material is arranged thematically, first in broad categories and then, by way of the indices at the back of the book, in a more detailed manner. When planning for children's work, it is advisable to read through the suggested Bible passages prayerfully. You are then in a better position to see how the programme relates to the theme, and also to supplement and vary the material as a result of your own insights and the specific needs of your group.

A few general ideas about storytelling:

- Tell the story from the viewpoint of the character in the situation. To create the time-machine effect, avoid eye contact as you slowly put on the appropriate cloth or cloak, and then make eye contact as you meet the children in character.

- Have an object with you which leads into the story – a water jug or lunch box, for instance.

- Walk the whole group through the story, so that they are physically moving from one place to another; and use all kinds of places, such as broom cupboards, under the stairs, outside under the trees, and so on. Needless to say, every care should be taken to ensure children's safety wherever you work with them.

- Collect some carpet tiles – blue and green – so that at story time the children can sit around the edge of these and help you position the cut outs for the story.

May God bless you all, and the children with whom you worship.

Susan Sayers

Contents

NEW LIFE IN CHRIST

Resources

Children's versions of Bible stories can be found in a number of publications in book and video format:

The Word for All Age Worship – 100 Bible stories retold for all age worship (Kevin Mayhew)
International Children's Bible – New Century Version (Word Publishing)
Children's Video Bible (still cartoons) (Lion)
The Big Book of All-time Bible Stories (Alpha)
Adventure Story Bible (Bible Society)

A number of songs are suggested for each session, and are generally taken from the following sources:

WUW   *Wake up, World! – Twenty-five songs about God's wonderful creation* (Kevin Mayhew)
WW   *Wonderful World! Christian Assemblies for Primary Schools* (Kevin Mayhew)
CAP   *Come and Praise* (Complete edition) (BBC)
A   *Alleluya! 77 songs for thinking people* (A & C Black)
GWP   *God's Wonderful People – More Christian Assemblies for Schools* (Kevin Mayhew)

Other songs, for which no specific source is given, are generally available in a range of song and hymn books.
Songs on tape are also extremely useful, such as the following:

Ishmael: Children's Praise Party Series (Kingsway)
Wake up, World! – Twenty-five songs about God's wonderful creation (Kevin Mayhew)
Kids' Praise (Spring Harvest, ICC)

GOD OUR CREATOR AND REDEEMER

Who Made . . . ?

Things to Read

Psalm 104
Genesis 1
Revelation 21: 1-7, 22-end

Things to Do

Aim: To help the children sense something of God's creative power.

Play the 'Who made the ice cream?' game, so that they can see that, however man-made something appears, if you trace it back it begins with God. The children like to challenge this claim and can usually think of some pretty unlikely starting points. You can chart their ideas like this:

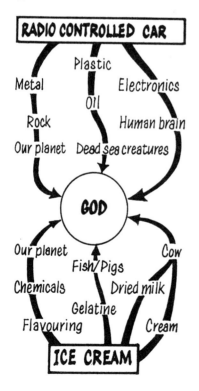

This leads on to the obvious question – who made God? Such a deep question is often asked by quite young children and we can delight with them in the mind-blowing answer: nobody made God! God always was, always is and always will be.

Now spend some time examining with magnifying glasses some of the clever designs this amazing alive-for-ever God thinks up. Have a selection of natural objects and pass them round in small groups getting everyone to notice something different about each object. This encourages the children to look really carefully and become more sensitive to the details of design in things which we often take for granted. Your selection of objects might include: a piece of evergreen, a stone, a twig of rose-hips, an apple, a cabbage leaf, the child's own hand. All the objects could be brought into church and displayed, with the title: Our God is wise and loving.

Things to Sing

God is making a wonderful world (WUW)
God made the earth (WUW)
Morning has broken (CAP)
Somebody greater (CAP)
Think of a world (CAP)
Let it be! (GWP)

God Can Do Anything

Things to Read

Psalm 104
Job 38:1-21; 42:1-6
Acts 14:8-17

Things to Sing

God is making a wonderful world (WUW)
God made the earth (WUW)
Carpenter, carpenter (CAP)
God who made the earth (CAP)

Things to Do

Aim: To help the children understand that when we're being loving we are passing on God's love.

Show and talk about something you have managed to make, but which you needed a bit of help with. Let the children share about something they have made and are really proud of. Talk together about how nice it is when you get to a really tricky bit if someone is there to help you out.

In the centre of the circle, have a few children to help you tell the story by acting it out. Now narrate the Acts reading, from the healing of the lame man through to the people thinking Paul and Barnabas had done the healing themselves. Stop and ask the children what they think – if it wasn't them, then who had made the man better?

Can God really do something as amazing as that?

Thank the volunteer actors and lay out in the circle lots of pictures of our beautiful creation – from stars and planets to tiny insects. Put on some music while you and the children wander round very quietly, thanking God for each thing he has made.

Now we can see that God is so great that anything is possible for him, no matter how difficult it may seem for us.

Seeing God Through People

Things to Read

Psalm 66:1-9
Exodus 1:8-14,22-2:10
Hebrews 3:1-6

Things to Do

Aim: To help the children see the difference between looking at God's creation and looking through it to God.

Have plenty of coloured cellophane toffee wrappers (you may need to eat some toffees first). Ask everyone to look at their wrapper carefully and tell one another what they can see on it. There may be the odd sticky patches, wrinkly bits, creases, slits or specks of dust.

Now try looking through the wrappers and notice how everything changes colour. If there is time, let them swap the wrappers around to see all the different colours.

Tell the story of Moses with the help of some visual aids and willing actors, drawing the story from the children if they are already familiar with it. Explain how we can look at Moses and learn a lot from him (just as we looked straight at our wrappers) but we can also find that, as Moses was God's friend, looking at his life helps us see God in a new way (as we saw everything differently when we looked through our wrappers).

Make this model using toffee paper and card.

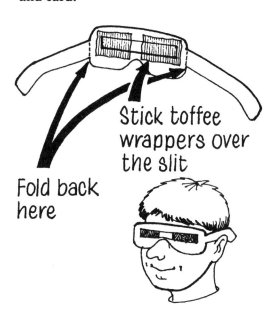

Stick toffee wrappers over the slit

Fold back here

Things to Sing

Give me oil in my lamp
Kum ba yah
Love is his word (A)

10

God Saves His People

Things to Read

Psalm 34:1-7
Zechariah 8:1-7
Acts 15:1-21

Things to Sing

God is making a wonderful world (WUW)
Give me oil in my lamp
Come on and celebrate
You shall go out with joy

Things to Do

Aim: To help the children understand God's delight in restoration.

You will require something which the church needs to have mended, sorted out or re-covered (such as an old notice board, an area of the churchyard, a general tip which could be a useful cupboard) and cleaning/repairing materials.

Tell the children about the people of Israel messing up their side of the covenant with God and eventually ending up as exiles. Link this with how we feel when we've messed things up and landed ourselves in trouble. Introduce someone as the prophet, who has a message for them all. (If this person is a clear reader, she/he can read out a simplified version of the prophecy her/himself.) God loves his people and promises to restore them to their own country. His message makes people hopeful again. God doesn't enjoy punishing us – what he enjoys is helping us put things right.

Now tackle the restoration work yourselves, singing as you do so, and enjoy working on it.

God Loves All that He has Made

Things to Read

Psalm 132:13-16
Isaiah 40:18-end

Things to Do

Aim: To help the children appreciate the greatness and majesty of God.

You will need a number of wildlife magazines, calendars and seed catalogues for cutting up, scissors, glue, pens and a large sheet of card; also some reference books with good pictures of the universe and our planet viewed from space. A few percussion instruments may be used too.

First, look at the reference books together, helping the children imagine the size and beauty of the universe God has made. Then make a working model of the solar system using one child to be the sun and nine others of varying size to be the planets. These children move slowly round the sun in their orbits while any remaining children play some quiet 'space music'. Or everyone can sing a worship song such as 'All that I am' (Spring Harvest – *Kids' Praise 1992*)

Then help the children to make a collage picture of the beauty of our created universe, including on it written truths about God, such as 'Our God loves what he has made'; 'Heaven and earth are full of his glory'.

Things to Sing

All that I am (*Kids' Praise 1992* – Spring Harvest)
God is making a wonderful world (WUW)
God made the earth (WUW)
All things bright and beautiful
Somebody greater (CAP)

We Believe

Things to Read

Daniel 5
Acts 25:1-12

Things to Do

Aim: For the children to see how Paul's reaction to his hardship showed that Jesus was Lord of his life.

First play the 'Simon says' game, in which they have to listen out for the authority of 'Simon' before carrying out the orders.

If possible have a man to tell Paul's story from Paul's point of view, putting on the appropriate headgear to do so. If you have no men on the team, try to borrow someone for the morning. Whoever does the telling will need to prepare the story from Acts 20 where Paul goes to Jerusalem and the Jews attack him. The children can be brought into the story as Paul's enemies. Have a question time afterwards, with the children questioning Paul (still in character) about his adventures.

Point out that what made the religious leaders so angry was that Paul was saying that Jesus was Lord – that a human was God. It is an amazing thing to claim, but it's true. Go over the things Jesus did which made it clear that Jesus really is the Christ everyone had been waiting for, and try this simple creed. The responses need to be really loud.

Who was there before anyone else?
GOD WAS!

Who created the entire universe?
GOD DID!

Who is in charge of the universe today?
GOD IS!

Who was walking the earth as Jesus?
GOD WAS!

Who loves us so much that he died for us all?
GOD DOES!

Who is alive for ever and living in his people?
GOD IS!

Who do we believe in?
WE BELIEVE IN GOD!

Help the children to make some bracelets, anklets and neck bands to wear.

Things to Sing

He was born in the winter (WUW)
Out to the great wide world we go! (WUW)
The journey of life (CAP)
Love is his word (A)
Put your hand in the hand (A)

JESUS IS LORD...JESUS IS LORD...JESUS IS LORD

Bricks Without Straw

Things to Read

Psalm 119:105-112
Exodus 5:1-9

Things to Do

Aim: To teach the children this section of the Moses story, helping them to understand what was happening.

One way to start the session would be by asking the children to make brick jigsaws. You could divide them into groups and have a competition for who completes a certain number of them first. Time how long it takes for each group to have all their bricks 'made'. Now emphasise the impossibility of Pharaoh's command by giving the same task, except that this time the pieces of jigsaw are taken to different parts of the room before everyone begins, so they need to be collected before everyone can start. Stop everyone at the time they completed the task the first time. They will be able to imagine the frustration the people felt, being punished for failing where they couldn't possibly achieve.

Alternatively, give out beanbags and divide the children into equal groups. First they stand in circles with one person in the middle who throws the beanbag to each group member in turn. Next they have to take the same amount of time to do the same things, except that they first have to find the hidden beanbag.

Now tell the story of Moses, Pharaoh and the bricks without straw. Have some words describing feelings printed on card and scattered on the floor. Have three hoops (or lengths of string) labelled MOSES, PHARAOH and THE PEOPLE OF ISRAEL. Discuss how each might have felt, putting the word cards in the appropriate hoops. Some may overlap, in a Venn diagram, like this:

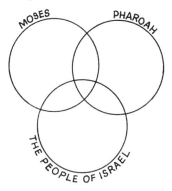

Here are some suggested words to describe their feelings:
angry, depressed, lonely, irritated, threatened, selfish, determined, embarrassed, sad, cheated, puzzled.

Things to Sing

Pick up your feet and go! (WUW)
Moses, I know you're the man
Make me a channel of your peace
Black and white (CAP)
The family of man (CAP)

God is Loving and Merciful

Things to Read

Psalm 19
Mark 9:33-37

Things to Do

Aim: For the children to understand that God's nature is loving and merciful.

Have a selection of shapes for the children to handle and make patterns with. You can buy sets of plastic or wooden shapes or you can make them as a resource from coloured card.

When the children have experienced the shapes, ask them to close their eyes, pick one up, guess what it is and then open their eyes to check if they were right, and let this lead on to what it is about a circle or square which makes them easy to tell apart. Can a circle ever be a square? Can a triangle ever be round? No. It's their nature to be the kind of shape they are.

What's God's nature? Jot up their ideas on a chart and keep asking, 'How do you know?' Have some Bibles and illustrated Bible stories at hand to show God's nature in action.

Now help the children to make this moving model (opposite). The qualities which come round into the mind bubble could be taken from what the children have just been talking about, or they can be these, which are like Jesus expressing his thoughts:

- we all need to love one another.
- don't be afraid – I am with you.
- trust me – I will never let you down.
- I will be with you always.
- I forgive you – go in peace.

Things to Sing

I'm black, I'm white, I'm short, I'm tall (WUW)
Jesus had all kinds of friends (WUW)
Out to the great wide world we go! (WUW)
Love is his word (A)
Lord of the dance
He's got the whole world in his hand

Learning Obedience

Things to Read

1 Samuel 8:4-22a
Mark 12:13-17

Things to Sing

God is making a wonderful world (WUW)
Pick up your feet and go! (WUW)
Lord of the dance

Things to Do

Aim: For the children to learn about obedience to God and to those who look after us.

Have everyone moving round the room in the ways you direct – forwards, backwards, sideways, slowly, quickly etc. From time to time tell them to stop and then go again. Talk about obeying orders and making an effort to do this without arguing! Talk about how difficult it is to obey when you really want to do something else instead, and suggest ways to improve this for everyone. (Asking for it to be made known what is to be the final deadline for finishing a game; having a family rota for house jobs, so that everyone agrees what is fair; deciding in advance on bedtimes, getting up times and hair wash days.)

Pray together for our own world leaders. Then everyone can help make a large painting of all kinds of different places we come across in our lives. Over each is stamped or stuck a JESUS IS LORD.

In the playground

At home

In the car

Praising God in Times of Trouble

Things to Read

Psalm 130
Acts 16:16-end

Things to Do

Aim: To introduce the children to the story of Paul and Silas in prison.

Have a few balls and chains made from card circles and paper chains made with black or shiny paper. Prison bars can be oven shelves, held up in front of the prisoners.

Begin by asking the children to share memories of some of the worst times in their lives and how they felt during those times. Then tell or read the story of Paul and Silas, with the children making the appropriate sound for the whipping and the doors clanging shut. Have some of the children fastened up with the balls and chains, and then think how Paul and Silas must have felt. Yet they sang! (The children can sing their favourite songs at this point.) Have some using instruments such as shakers, drums and cymbals to create the earthquake, and call out above the noise as Paul did, so that the children can sense the panic and confusion with Paul in control.

After the story, (which the children may well want to do twice to get it really lifelike) talk about how we can sing our praises in those worst times, knowing that God is good, even if we are in a sticky patch, and giving God praise in those times is one of the best presents we can give him.

Have a time of prayer for all those who are in prison for their beliefs at the moment, and help the children make these balls and chains to take home.

Things to Sing

Out to the great wide world we go! (WUW)
Pick up your feet and go! (WUW)
In the winter, nights are dark (WUW)
Give me oil in my lamp
Morning has broken

God Brings Good out of Evil

Things to Read

Psalm 81
Genesis 50:15-24
1 John 2:1-12

Things to Do

Aim: To help the children look at choosing God's way of behaving.

Start by playing a quick game, such as crab football where you all move around like this:

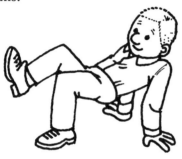

Talk together about the way we keep having to make choices in a game, and we sometimes know we've made bad decisions and messed things up. That's also true in life. Have a joint telling of the Joseph story – the part where the brothers had decided to get rid of Joseph. So the brothers had really messed things up for Joseph. Or had they? Explain how God always works to bring some good out of our mistakes. Can the children think of any good that came out of what the brothers had done? Make a list of their suggestions, then tell or read what happened when the brothers' father had died, pausing to let them guess how Joseph will react to the story. (The children may well recognise the temptation to twist the truth to get out of trouble!) Then go on to see what Joseph actually said.

Help them to make this choosing chart and try it out on their friends and family.

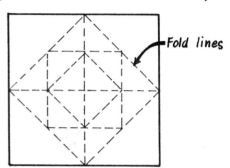

Fold lines

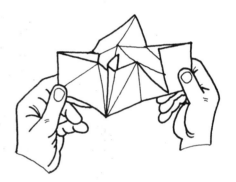

Things to Sing

God is making a wonderful world (WUW)
Keep on travelling on (WUW)
When I needed a neighbour (CAP)
Love is his word (A)

The Nature of God

Things to Read

Psalm 29
Exodus 34:1-10
Acts 2:22-36

Things to Do

Aim: To help the children understand more about God's nature.

Have a large sheet of paper entitled: 'What we know about God'. A long strip of lining or wall paper is ideal, and the larger the paper the larger their writing can be. Sit all along both sides of the paper, with a variety of felt tip pens available. Talk together about what God is like, and have every right idea written down colourfully on the paper. If they need some help, see what they can work out from the way the universe is created, the way we are created, the way Jesus behaved and the way God's friends behave.

Have some quiet music playing as all the characteristics of God are read out in turn. Compare these with what Peter says in his post-Pentecost sermon and with what Moses knew of God. Phrases from the psalms can be used instead.

Using felt tips, stickers or paints and photos, fill in the areas between the words so that the whole sheet of paper is a blaze of colour expressing the character of God.

Things to Sing

I'm black, I'm white, I'm short, I'm tall (WUW)
Out to the great wide world we go! (WUW)
God is love, his the care
Love is his word (A)
Give me oil in my lamp

GOD WITH US

Joy and Anger

Things to Read

Jeremiah 7:1-11
Luke 19:29-end

Things to Do

Aim: To see the contrast between the joy of the entry into Jerusalem and the anger of Jesus at the abuse of the temple.

First, make pom-poms, as shown:

1. Cut a handful of lengths of different coloured crepe paper

2. Fold it in the middle

3. Put two rubber bands on it like this

Use the pom-poms either in an all age procession or in a time of singing and dancing with the children on their own.

Then tell the story of Jesus throwing out the money changers, acting it as you tell it, explaining how the temple was being misused and then literally overturning a few tables and spilling everything onto the floor. The shock of seeing and hearing this really helps them realise the depth of Jesus' concern to put things right.

Things to Sing

Out to the great wide world we go! (WUW)
Come on and celebrate

Following the Star

Things to Read

Psalm 8
Isaiah 42:1-9
Matthew 2:1-12

Things to Do

Aim: For the children to look at the different ways God leads us in our spiritual journey.

Beforehand, set up the secret worship place which is where the trail will end. It might be a large cupboard or under-stair area, a small vestry or even a tent. Whatever you choose, it needs to be out of sight when the children start their trail. Set the children off in groups on a trail, either inside or out depending on the weather. Each group follows their own trail of coloured stars, which are placed far enough apart for there to be times when the direction is uncertain until they look more carefully (rather like cairns on mountains).

Each group's journey eventually leads to the same finishing point. This worship area is beautiful. It may have flowers placed on a mirror, lights or candles (great care!) an open Bible and a cross. Have a rug or blanket down on the floor and quiet music playing, and make the entrance low so that they have to stoop to go in. The idea is to make it a secret place of wonder which they are led to find. Have a SILENCE notice outside, and make sure the children come in quietly. When everyone is crowded inside, tell them quietly and simply how God led the wise men to find him, and he leads us to find him as well. But we don't all come by the same route. God uses all the different events of our lives, and the different people we meet; he can use sad times as well as happy times.

Sing a worship song together that the children know well, and then pray for people who are going through different bits of their journey at the moment. Have music playing again as the children file out and colour this star prayer to hang up at home.

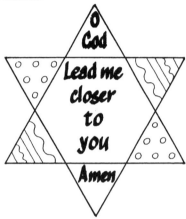

Things to Sing

Keep on travelling on (WUW)
Pick up your feet and go! (WUW)
I'm black, I'm white, I'm short, I'm tall (WUW)
Ride that camel! Chase that star! (WW)
One more step along the world I go
The journey of life (CAP)
I want to see your baby boy (CAP)

Getting Ready for Jesus

Things to Read

Isaiah 40:1-11
Luke 1:5-25

Things to Do

Aim: To introduce the children to John the Baptist.

Begin by enlisting everyone's help in getting the place ready for painting. When that is done, point out how we needed to change things in the room, putting them in new places, so that the room was ready. Today we are going to look at someone who helped people prepare their lives so they would be ready to meet Jesus.

Now tell the story of Zechariah and Elizabeth, adding that when the baby grew up he did just what the angel had said – he helped people get ready for Jesus. Ask them to think of one thing in their lives which they know is not right – telling lies, not going to bed when they're told, being rude, not sharing, being a bad loser etc. and suggest they try and tackle that one thing.

Use the paints to make a large picture of John the Baptist baptising people in the Jordan. Call it: GETTING READY FOR JESUS.

Things to Sing

God is making a wonderful world (WUW)
Out to the great wide world we go! (WUW)
In the winter nights are dark (WUW)
Give me oil in my lamp
Kum ba yah

Mary and Elizabeth

Things to Read

Psalm 40
1 Samuel 1:1-20
Luke 1:26-45

Things to Do

Aim: To meet some people who worked with God by trusting him.

Beforehand, prepare card pictures of Zechariah, Elizabeth, Joseph and Mary. Elizabeth and Mary are both looking very happy. Also make signposts which say 'To Nazareth', and 'Elizabeth's house'. Put down the story mat, or green and blue sheets/carpet tiles.

Get the children to tell the story of Gabriel visiting Mary to tell her that she would have a son who would save his people. (This is something most will be familiar with already.) Point out how Mary said she was happy for it all to happen God's way, and how Joseph was prepared to marry her and help her look after the baby.

Now tell the children about Mary's cousin, Elizabeth; the way she had prayed for a child and was now six months pregnant with John, and how her husband had been told by an angel that his son would prepare the way for Jesus.

Using the story mat and figures, with the children adding trees and paths, tell how Mary went to visit her cousin, and what happened when they met. (Those with baby brothers and sisters may remember how babies move around in the womb.)

Help the children make these cards to remind them to say 'Yes' to God.

Front

 Push in split pin to form a handle not at the front but at the BACK of the door.

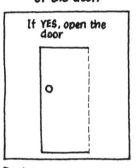

Back

Things to Sing

Kum ba yah
Give me oil in my lamp
The Virgin Mary had a baby boy (CAP)

Jesus Will Come Again

Things to Read

Psalm 40
Jeremiah 33:10-16
Revelation 21:1-6

Things to Do

Aim: To help children understand that Christians look both forwards and backwards.

Talk about going back to times we have enjoyed – you could show some holiday snaps to give them the idea. Ask them to think back to their last summer holiday and then forward to the things they want to do again next time.

As Christians, we look back to the time when Jesus lived among us as a human person. We also look forward to the time he has promised to come back again. (To many children this comes as a great surprise and they have lots of questions about it. Answer them without surmising anything, recognising that even Jesus himself didn't know when it would be, but we do know it will happen, whether we are alive or dead at the time.)

Help them make this model to remember that we are preparing for both events.

Things to Sing

Keep on travelling on (WUW)
Out to the great wide world we go! (WUW)
Lord of the dance

Colour yourself,
fold flap and fix
dot to dot with split pin

Move the person
to look back at the crib and
forward to the second coming.

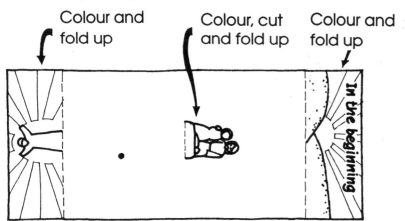

Colour and fold up   Colour, cut and fold up   Colour and fold up

In the beginning

God is a Great Builder!

Things to Read

Psalm 132
Haggai 2:1-9
1 Peter 2:1-10

Things to Do

Aim: To help the children see that God works in us to put things right where they have gone wrong.

You will need a number of cartons and boxes and other interesting junk to build with, plenty of sticky tape and parcel tape, staples and pens.

First remind the children of how smart King Solomon's temple had been. Get them to make the temple with their bodies, bit by bit, like this:

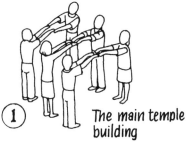

① The main temple building

② The tall pillars

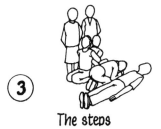

③ The steps

Now explain how after many years of the people's being unfaithful to God, the temple was attacked and reduced to rubble. (Everyone falls down.) Many people were taken off to Babylon.

Then after seventy years, the people were allowed to return, and all they found was their beautiful temple in ruins. As the children lie there, read them Haggai's words and then let them slowly rebuild themselves. Tell them how God can rebuild us whenever we fall down through doing or thinking or saying what is unloving or evil, and help them use some apparently useless junk to build a superb structure.

Things to Sing

God is making a wonderful world (WUW)
Out to the great wide world we go (WUW)
He's got the whole world in his hand

Thank God for Families!

Things to Read

Isaiah 43:1-13
Matthew 2

Things to Do

Aim: To teach children about the dangers of Jesus' early life and God's protection through his family.

You will need colouring pens, scissors, staples and copies of the model pieces illustrated; also slips of paper with the names of different members of animal families – enough to cover the number in the group. First play the 'animal families' game. Each child is shown a slip of paper which has on it the daddy, mummy or baby form of an animal. When everyone knows who they are they have to find the other members of their family by making the right noises. When they are a family, Daddy stands behind a chair, Mummy sits on the chair and the baby sits on Mummy's lap!

Now praise God and thank him for our families, remembering each person we live with. Tell the children the dangers of Jesus' early life, and how he escaped because of Joseph hearing God's warning and rushing his family off – perhaps in the middle of the night – as refugees. (*Donkeys' Glory* by Nan Goodall includes a classic retelling of this episode). Help the children to catch the very real danger and fear there must have been, and the support of the family in the time of peril.

Help the children make this stand-up model of the journey into Egypt.

Things to Sing

Ride that camel! Chase that star! (WW)
Keep on travelling on (WUW)
Pick up your feet and go! (WUW)
I'm black, I'm white, I'm short, I'm tall (WUW)
I want to see your baby boy (CAP)
Kum ba yah

The Importance of Being Ready

Things to Read

Isaiah 2:10-end
Matthew 24:1-14

Things to Sing

Out to the great wide world we go! (WUW)
Give me oil in my lamp

Things to Do

Aim: To explore getting ready and being ready.

Have some different types of work clothing, such as a judo suit, Brownie gear, school uniform, football strip, overall etc. Also have a house plant and watering can and/or a small pet.

As you get different children to dress up, talk about how we have to get prepared to do things, and we enjoy it while we're feeling keen. Then we might start getting fed up with it. (Get them to undress back into ordinary clothes again.) Even if we're actually still going along, we're rather lazy about it now.

Talk about the importance in our Christian life not only of getting ready but of keeping ready. Show the children the house plant and/or small pet – the getting ready is exciting but we also have to keep on with the feeding and watering and so on, or the plants and pets would die. If we want our faith to stay alive, we've got to look after that as well, feeding it with praying and reading the Bible. This would be a good opportunity to have a few different Bible reading schemes on show to look at, and on sale for parents afterwards.

Everyone's Special to God

Things to Read

1 Kings 10:1-13
John 4:1-26 or 1-42

Things to Do

Aim: For the children to know that in Jesus' eyes each one is special.

Start by playing the 'countdown' game. Everyone stands up and you say you're thinking of someone and they can find out who it is by asking questions. You can only answer 'yes' or 'no', and the one thing they can't ask is whether it's a particular person. The game is really a process of elimination, so if someone asks 'Is this person wearing glasses?' and the answer is 'yes', then everyone who isn't wearing glasses sits down. Finally there is only one person standing, and that should be the one you were thinking of.

Talk with the children about how God knows all the details about us and understands us really well. That makes him the very best person to trust with our worries and secrets, our successes and struggles.

Give the children this chart to fill in, which they don't have to show to anyone at all; in fact one way of doing this is by asking them to go and find a place of their choice, either indoors or, if possible, outside. Tell them that when you want them back you will ring a bell. When you are all together again, ask them to hold their charts containing their own special information as you all pray in silence for one another, knowing that at the same time each is being prayed for by someone else.

My best colour is [ ]
My best food is [ ]
What makes me scared
[ ]
What makes me happy
[ ]
What I like best about me
[ ]
What I don't like about me
[ ]

Things to Sing

I'm black, I'm white, I'm short, I'm tall (WUW)
Out to the great wide world we go! (WUW)
Well, Well, Well! (WW)
Stand up! Walk tall! (WW)
Black and white (CAP)
The family of man (CAP)
It's me, O Lord (A)

The Ministry of Jesus

Vision for a Blind Man

Things to Read

Psalm 139:1-18
John 9:1-7

Things to Do

Aim: To teach the story of the blind man being healed.

Begin with a game not using your eyes, such as 'pinning the tail on the donkey' or 'squeak, piggy, squeak'.

Talk together about how difficult it is when you can't see, and then tell the story from today's gospel, either using the floor tiles method or acting the story out as you tell it, with everyone moving to different parts of the room for the different parts of the story.

Then help the children make this model with moving eyes to remind them of the passage they have been hearing about.

Things to Sing

Jesus had all kinds of friends (WUW)
Out to the great wide world we go! (WUW)
Lord of the dance
God who made the earth (CAP)
He's got the whole world in his hand

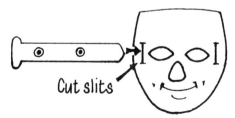

Cut slits

Cut out eyes
and nose

Jesus on Trial

Things to Read

Isaiah 53:1-5
Matthew 26:57-end

Things to Do

Aim: To look at Jesus' arrest and persecution, addressing the question of why such a good person was treated so badly.

First show the children these messages and ask them to read them.

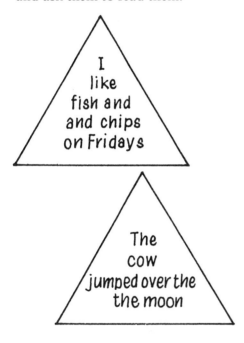

They will probably read them without noticing the repetition because they are not expecting it. We tend to see what we expect to see: many faithful Jews expected Christ to be like another King David, and thought that he would lead his people to fight against the Romans so that they would be freed from Roman rule. Jesus wasn't like that, and talked about his kingdom in a very different way, so many people didn't recognise him as the Christ.

Now give out 'Happy Family' cards and play a round of this game, where you can ask one person if they have a particular card and they have to answer honestly. Warn the children that in the story Jesus will be asked a question, and you want them to listen out for what he replied.

Now tell or read the passage from Matthew using pictures from a children's Bible. Or a few of the young people could come and act it out in a simple way. Afterwards, talk about the question Jesus was asked.

Now help them to make this three dimensional scene of the court and Jesus looking at Peter.

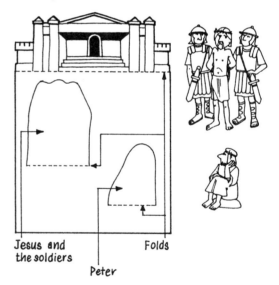

Jesus and the soldiers   Folds

Peter

Things to Sing

He was born in a stable (WUW)
You can't pin Jesus down (WUW)
Lord of the dance
Jesus Christ is here (CAP)

Jesus Sets Us Free

Things to Read

Psalm 56
Luke 13:10-17

Things to Do

Aim: To explore how Jesus gives us freedom.

Tell the story of the crippled lady being healed on the Sabbath in the synagogue. You could do this by acting out the crowd watching, the Pharisees watching and Jesus calling out to the woman – she wasn't standing next to him. Look closely at the details of the account so that you get the real atmosphere rather than a clinical 'Jesus trick'.

Divide the children into teams. One child from each team is caged in with chairs and can only be released by a special combination lock which the rest of the team have to solve. Whoever solves the combination first and releases their team member, wins.

Here is the muddled message:

SET IN LET YOU AND LOVE FREE HIS WILL JESUS

which they must unravel to say:

LET JESUS IN AND HIS LOVE WILL SET YOU FREE.

Things to Sing

I'm black, I'm white, I'm short, I'm tall (WUW)
Out to the great wide world we go! (WUW)
Stand up! Walk tall! (WW)
Give me oil in my lamp
He's got the whole world in his hand

Learn to Listen!

Things to Read

Deuteronomy 4:1-21
Luke 13:22-end

Things to Do

Aim: To look at the teaching aspect of Jesus' ministry.

Beforehand prepare two simple sock puppets tied with string to the script so that children will be able to read it.

Cathy Dad, you know the hose pipe?

Dad Hang on, Cathy, I'm rather busy. I've got to get the garden watered before lunch.

Cathy But Dad, that's what I mean, the hose pipe is . . .

Dad Cathy, I said I was busy. You run off and play.

Cathy O.K. Dad, but I wish you would listen.

Dad In a minute, love. Right, I'll just turn on and . . . AAAHHH! The hose is leaking and the water is soaking me!

Cathy Yes, Dad, I knew it was going to do that. I could see the hole in the hose pipe.

Dad Then why didn't you tell me, you rotter!

Ask two confident readers to make the puppets act out the sketch, and then talk about how Cathy's dad could have avoided getting really soaked. Sometimes we could all save ourselves a lot of trouble by listening to one another better. Jesus went around talking to people and listening to them and explaining how their lives could be freed from all the guilt and fear which worried them so much. Lots of people listened and learnt from what Jesus said. He helped them sort their lives out. But lots of others were too tied up with their own ideas really to hear what Jesus was saying – they listened with a bit of themselves, but didn't really listen deep down, so they missed out. At this point the children can read the passage from Luke.

Help the children make this jigsaw to complete before a certain time is up (depending on the age and ability of the children).

Things to Sing

God made the earth (WUW)
Out to the great wide world we go! (WUW)
When Jesus walked in Galilee (CAP)
Love is his word (A)

A Story with a Secret

Things to Read

Psalm 128 or 133
Isaiah 5:1-7
John 15:1-11

Things to Sing

Out to the great wide world we go! (WUW)
Love is his word (A)
When Jesus walked in Galilee (CAP)

Things to Do

Aim: To explore the nature of a parable.

First talk about secrets and keeping special things in secret places. Now tell them a parable – a story which has a secret hidden inside. (It's the story of the vine growing grapes and the branches that are cut off being unable to grow any.) Tell the story with a plant that has a good root system, either brought inside or with the children gathered around a plant outside. Cut a branch off at the appropriate time.

Try and work out what the secret meaning of the story is. They may be able to think of the secrets in other parables that they know such as the lost sheep.

Now help the children make this model of what a parable is which they can use to keep their own secrets inside.

You will need a box

Inside you will need cotton wool

and things to decorate it

PASTA TWIRLS

and spray paint

and a secret

Being a Friend

Things to Read

Jeremiah 33:10-11
Luke 7:36-end

Things to Do

Aim: To think about what makes a good friend.

Use puppets to act out different situations where the children decide whether there's a good friend or not. Make some of these very obvious, such as comforting and sharing situations, but make some more subtle, such as a disagreement where the puppets argue and end up laughing. It is important that children realise we are talking about the real world and not some cloud cuckoo land. They need to know that they can trust Jesus with their grumpy and angry times as well as with the times they are feeling good.

Make a list of all their ideas about what makes a good friend and point out how Jesus is all of these and more: he is the best friend we could ever wish to have.

Things to Sing

Jesus had all kinds of friends (WUW)
I'm black, I'm white, I'm short, I'm tall (WUW)
Out to the great wide world we go! (WUW)
Magic penny (A)
Make me a channel of your peace

Jesus and the Law

Things to Read

1 Samuel 21:1-6
Matthew 12:1-13

Things to Do

Aim: Jesus shows up what the law really means.

Start with a picture which you have covered with lots of pieces of paper, labelled with letters. Taking it in turns, the children ask for a letter to be removed and they see how quickly they can discover what the picture is. Only when all the bits are removed will the picture be clear to see.

Remind everyone of the ten commandments, either in full or in Jesus' summary of the law in Matthew 22:37-40, and then have a couple of leaders or helpers being Pharisees telling the children some bad gossip about Jesus disobeying the law in various ways ('harvesting' food and healing someone on the Sabbath). What do the children think? Are the Pharisees right? It's true that Jesus did these things. Was he being disobedient to God's law?

When they have had a chance to think about that, read how Jesus answered the Pharisees' complaints.

Then let the children do this puzzle.

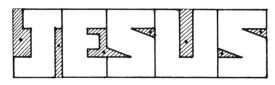

1. Colour in the dotted parts.
2. Cut these parts out.
3 Try to make them into Jesus' name on a plain sheet of paper.

Things to Sing

He was born in the winter (WUW)
Out to the great wide world we go! (WUW)
Love is his word (A)
One more step along the world I go

35

Love and Law

Things to Read

Psalm 136:1-9
Nehemiah 13:15-22
John 5:1-21

Things to Do

Aim: To help the children see the difference between keeping God's law and not getting bogged down in petty rules.

You will need two large cartons and some strips of card about as long as the boxes are tall. Beforehand cover the boxes on one side and write out the summary of the law on them: *Love God*, and *Love one another*. On the long strips write things like: *Don't carry your mat on the Sabbath; You must not walk more than a short way on the Sabbath; You must do this; you must not do that.*

First sing the summary of the law to the tune of *London's Burning* with actions, as follows:

You shall love the
    (hands on heart)

Lord your God with
    (point up, hand open)

all your heart and
    (one hand on heart)

all your mind and
    (both hands hold head)

all your strength
    (clench fists and show biceps)

all your strength!
and love your neighbour
    (one arm round shoulder of next person)

and love your neighbour
    (one arm round person on other side)

This can be sung as a round, of course.

Have the boxes displayed, and then explain how all the other rules were added to the law to protect it. The children can get these rules and lean them up against the Law until we can't see it very well any more.

Now tell the story of Jesus healing the man on the Sabbath and pause when he picks up his mat. What do they think the synagogue teachers will think about that? Point out how they had protected the Law so well that they had lost sight of its real meaning. Jesus swept away the clutter (let someone do this) to see the important part again.

Help the children make this model to remind them.

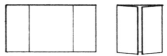

(1) Fold thin card like this

(2) Cut into the side flaps

(3) On the middle section write and decorate the law

(4) On the side flaps write 'Jesus shows us what is important.'

Things to Sing

Jesus had all kinds of friends (WUW)
Out to the great wide world we go! (WUW)
Love is his word (A)
It's me, O Lord (A)

Trusting God

Things to Read

Psalm 25:1-14
Jeremiah 17:5-14
John 10:11-15

Things to Do

Aim: We can trust God to save us.

Play a trust game first. One idea is for the children to get into pairs, with one of the pair blindfolded. The blindfolded person is then led round an obstacle course.

Afterwards discuss with the children how they needed to trust their partner for the game, otherwise they would have been in danger of getting hurt. Talk about times they have felt let down by people, and recognise that because we are weak as humans, we can't expect humans never to let us down, however difficult or frightening life gets.

Show the children a length of cotton contrasted with a length of really strong rope. They can try pulling on each. God is like the strong rope, and whenever they feel frightened or lonely, or tempted to do something cruel, they can hang on tight to the strong rope of God's love and it will never let them down.

Things to Sing

Pick up your feet and go! (WUW)
Jesus had all kinds of friends (WUW)
Out to the great wide world we go! (WUW)
Put your hand in the hand (A)
One more step along the world I go

Recognising Jesus

Things to Read

Psalm 136:1-9
Isaiah 26:1-9
John 4:43-end

Things to Do

Aim: To help the children recognise Jesus' glory through his signs.

You will need some ready-made icing mixture and a variety of fillings, such as chocolate drops, hundreds and thousands, or cherries.

First play the 'Who am I?' game:

Begin by talking about how first impressions are sometimes spot on, and sometimes disastrously wrong. We gradually get to know who someone really is by the clues their words and behaviour give us. Ask a volunteer (of twelve years or over) to come and help. Secretly show them the picture of what they are and then hang it on their back so that no one can see it. Invite everyone to ask the volunteer questions to which she/he can only answer 'yes' or 'no'. Keep track of what is found out until eventually the identity is guessed correctly and the volunteer turns round to reveal that she/he is indeed who they thought.

An alternative version of this is to ask the children to guess by gradually adding dressing up clues to the volunteer, such as whiskers, tail and ears, until the identity is revealed.

What on earth has this to do with our theme?

The fact is that we get to know Jesus in exactly the same way – bit by bit we start to discover his character by seeing how he acts towards people in the Gospel. Bit by bit, we learn that he is revealing God's nature to us until eventually we can say for certain that he truly is the Son of God.

Now tell the story of healing when Jesus didn't even actually touch the man's son, and notice how the man is convinced when he realises the timing of the boy's recovery. Point out our need to look if we are to see God's glory at work in our lives, and pray about this.

Help the children make these sweets which look quite ordinary but have a surprise in the centre.

Things to Sing

Jesus had all kinds of friends (WUW)
Out to the great wide world we go! (WUW)
This little light of mine (A)
Come on and celebrate

What is God Like?

Things to Read

Job 28:9-end
Luke 6:27-36

Things to Do

Aim: To recognise what God is like and see his characteristics reflected in people who love him.

First, play a game. Work out the number of pairs of children there are, and mix up that number of pairs of animals – a parent and a baby. Show each person the name or picture of one animal. Without using any animal noises, the children have to act out their animal until they find their pairs. They carry on miming their animals until everyone is paired up. Suitable animals for this game are: rabbits, elephants, birds, kangaroos, snakes, lions and horses.

Explain how people should be able to recognise us as God's children by the way we behave. What do they think God is like? Write down all the suggestions in bright colours on a poster. (This is one of those times when you may end up learning more than you expected to!)

Have a lively praise song to celebrate God being as he is and follow it with a short 'sorry' time of quietness, remembering when we haven't behaved like God our Father.

Help them to make a zigzag book by sticking a different quality of God's nature on each page. If there is time they can add others of their own.

Things to Sing

I'm black, I'm white, I'm short, I'm tall (WUW)
Out to the great wide world we go! (WUW)
Come on and celebrate
This little light of mine (A)
God knows me (CAP)

FAITH, TRUST, HOPE

Saying 'Yes' to God

Things to Read

Psalm 36:5-11
Genesis 18:1-19

Things to Do

Aim: To learn about choosing and responding.

Tell the children today's story about Abraham receiving his guests and being told that although he and his wife are old they are going to have a son. Point out how God had chosen Abraham for something which must have seemed pretty impossible, but his trust in God made it possible. Then follow a recipe together so that by following the instructions you end up with something nice to eat.

Things to Sing

Abraham! (WUW)
God is making a wonderful world (WUW)
One more step along the world I go
Give me oil in my lamp
The journey of life (CAP)

God is Our Hope

Things to Read

Psalm 23
Psalm 24
Psalm 78:1-24
Hebrews 10:19-25

Things to Do

Aim: For the children to know that with God nothing is impossible and we can put our hope in him.

Bring a vacuum cleaner in with you today.

Now ask someone to do a spot of vacuuming, but before they start ask the children how they know the vacuum will clear up the mess. Their trust in it will be based on past experience. (Try the cleaner to check that it really does work.) It is our past experience of God that makes us know he is worth trusting and can do the impossible in deadlock situations.

Take the children on a whistle stop tour of the wonders God performed (as in the psalm) in Egypt, and share any more recent wonders that have happened in your own experience.

Things to Sing

Pick up your feet and go! (WUW)
Keep on travelling on (WUW)
One more step along the world I go
Give me oil in my lamp

Begin with that excellent eating game, where you throw a dice in turn and when you get six you run up to the front, put on thick gloves and a scarf, and start to eat a chocolate bar with a knife and fork. As soon a someone else throws a six they take over.

After the game, talk about how we were all living hopefully as the dice came round, hoping that we would get a six. We are going to look at a hope which won't make any of us disappointed because we can all win.

God is the Centre of Our Lives

Things to Read

Psalm 42
Proverbs 14:31-15:17
James 4:13-5:11

Things to Do

Aim: For the children to understand the choices we have to make in the way we live.

In pairs play the 'Stone, paper, scissors' game where each child makes a choice at the same time and shows the appropriate hand sign. Stone wins over scissors (because it can break them), scissors win over paper (because they can cut it), and paper wins over stone (because it can wrap around it).

Now have the James passage written as if it is a real letter, in a stamped addressed envelope, and explain how James was writing to all the scattered Jewish Christians, and was very bothered about some unchristian behaviour. See if they can spot what this is. Use a translation such as the *International Children's Bible* where the shorter sentence structure makes it much easier to understand.

List all the things the children can remember, and then work out together how James really wants them to live. List the characteristics of a Christian life next to the bad things in a different colour.

Talk together about how hard it is to choose to live God's way. For instance, we may know we should be honest, but when we want to stay out of trouble and get frightened of what will happen if someone finds out what we've done, we really want to tell lies. Explain how we can ask Jesus to give us the courage to choose the right way, and he will help us.

Now help the children to make the model to remind them each day. They can choose which centre to put into their life – God or self.

Things to Sing

Out to the great wide world we go! (WUW)
Love is his word (A)
God is love, his the care
Magic penny (A)

1. Roll out self-hardening clay.

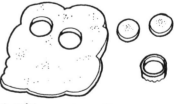

2. With a pastry cutter, cut out two 'plugs'.

3. Make and decorate a shape with a hole in the middle.

4. Write on one plug 'GOD' and on the other 'SELF'.

5. Keep the plugs next to the model. Each morning choose which plug to put in.

Thinking about Heaven

Things to Read

Daniel 10:2-19
Revelation 1:1-8

Things to Do

Aim: For the children to learn about heaven.

Strangely enough, one of the only parts of the Christian faith nominal Christians tell their children is that people (and often animals) are in heaven living with Jesus. It is, after all, a comforting story. Yet I find that in church this is the area least covered. If we don't talk much of this area of faith, children will sooner or later think of heaven as a baby story which they have to grow out of. So let's go for it, and bring all those secret questions into the open.

Start by asking the children what they think happens when a person's body wears out and dies. Listen carefully to their answers, so as to address any worries or misunderstandings you hear hinted at. Talk to them about what heaven is like, homing in on the qualities rather than on what it may or may not look like. What is important is that they begin to get a sense of a place which is happy, welcoming, loving and suitable for all ages! Make it clear that people do not turn into angels when they die, they won't have to hang around on clouds getting bored all day and it isn't somewhere you could reach by spaceship. Read to them Daniel's vision of heaven, and point out how lovingly Daniel is treated.

Then let them express their own ideas of heaven in painting, drawing, creative writing or clay.

Things to Sing

I'm black, I'm white, I'm short, I'm tall (WUW)
Keep on travelling on (WUW)
Jesus had all kinds of friends (WUW)
One more step along the world I go
Out to the great wide world we go! (WUW)

Don't Give Up

Things to Read

Jeremiah 38:1-13
James 1:1-12

Things to Sing

Keep on travelling on (WUW)
One more step along the world I go
Give me oil in my lamp

Things to Do

Aim: for the children to hear the story of Jeremiah and understand about not giving up.

Start with a fitness session of running on the spot, jumping, skipping and sit ups. While everyone relaxes, have some quiet music and talk about how hard it is sometimes to keep going on something we find difficult, but God will help us, often through our friends.

Tell the story of Jeremiah, using a large scale version of the model the children will be making. Then help the children to make a model of Jeremiah being pulled out of the muddy well. You will need a large plastic pot (yoghurt type), some plastic from other bottles and pots to cut Jeremiah out of, some bits of material, paper clips and scissors. Either make the sloshy mud yourselves by adding water to some earth from outside, or have this already made.

Paint outside
stone colour

YOGHURT

Mud inside

Thick cotton
thread

Paper clips to
weight

Recognising True Value

Things to Read

Psalm 119: 41-56
Nehemiah 8:1-12
Luke 11:37-end

Things to Do

Aim: For the children to hear Jesus' teaching to the Pharisees and look at real goodness.

Beforehand, gather a collection of some real and some pretend jewellery. Display it carefully so that it looks precious, and ask a couple of children to take it round and show everyone. If there are a lot of you, sing a quiet worship song while the jewels are doing the rounds.

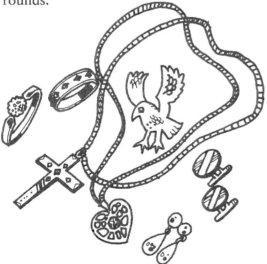

Talk with the children about which they thought were worth most, and why. Then let them in on the secret that some things were in the 50p range, though some of them may well have been taken in by them. It would only be when they broke easily or scratched that you'd realise with disappointment that they weren't as good as you'd thought. Some people are like this, too.

Now tell or read the story from Luke, getting the children to help you tell it by acting out the parts as you come to them. Explain first (and have them acting out) how fussy the Pharisees were about all the ceremonial washing; then they will notice how Jesus was far more bothered about the really important things than the rituals which were mainly just for show.

Then provide a number of different media so that they can choose how they want to express the story and teaching to the people in church. Some could act out the story in their own way, using the props from the teaching, some may wish to make a poster encouraging genuine Christianity.

Things to Sing

Jesus had all kinds of friends (WUW)
Out to the great wide world we go! (WUW)
I come like a beggar (CAP)
Love is his word (A)

A Journey of Faith

Things to Read

Psalm 37:1-6
Job 23:1-12
2 Corinthians 1:1-11

Things to Do

Aim: For the children to deepen their understanding of what faith means.

Beforehand, set up a length of wool around the room, or outside on a trail. First of all send people off in pairs to walk the trails. One of the pair is blindfold and holds on to the wool for guidance; the other person is there to encourage and direct, but not touch unless really necessary. Then swap round. This is an excellent exercise for noticing how vulnerable we feel when we can't see and don't know where we are going.

When everyone has had a go, talk together about how they felt and what scared them. In our faith we can't always see very clearly and have to feel our way through life bit by bit. But God has promised that those who seek will find, and he will always be there helping and guiding us and encouraging us as we go. Then help the children to make a sign which says JESUS IS LORD, which they can even read with their eyes shut because the letters are cut out of different materials.

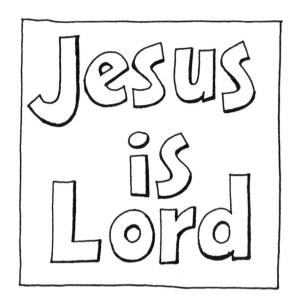

Things to Sing

Keep on travelling on (WUW)
Pick up your feet and go! (WUW)
Put your hand in the hand (A)
One more step along the world I go

Gideon Glorifies God

Things to Read

Psalm 93
Judges 7:1-8,19-23
John 7:1-24

Things to Do

Aim: For the children to understand the truth behind the Gideon story – faith shows in action; God knows what he's doing.

Begin with a 'sorting out' game, such as all those wearing yellow run to the back wall; all those who ate cornflakes for breakfast hop to the centre; all who watch 'Superman' leap across to the front wall etc.

Now tell the story of how God sorted out the soldiers and by following God closely Gideon cleverly led his army to victory. During the telling, hold a large version of the card the children will be making later, and break open the seal at the appropriate moment to reveal the light inside. We have a 'shepherds' fire' made for a nativity play which also comes in handy at different times of the year; if you have one hidden way, bring it out and use it for when Gideon creeps down to hear what the enemy are saying. These few props really focus attention, making the storytelling very realistic.

Then help the children to make the card model of the hidden lights. As you all work on the models, talk informally about how we need to keep looking and listening to God, so that we notice what he is trying to tell us. You may be able to share a personal example of revelation so that the children understand that it really happens even now.

Things to Sing

Out to the great wide world we go! (WUW)
The journey of life (CAP)
Give me oil in my lamp

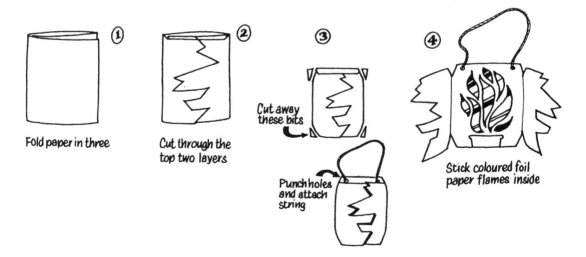

① Fold paper in three

② Cut through the top two layers

③ Cut away these bits
Punch holes and attach string

④ Stick coloured foil paper flames inside

Job's Perseverance

Things to Read

Job 1
2 Timothy 2:1-10

Things to Do

Aim: For the children to learn about the value of endurance and perseverance.

Start with a guessing game, such as 'I Spy', where we sometimes admit defeat and give up. As you are playing, notice whether people give up easily or keep pressing on, and mention this afterwards (without naming individuals of course).

Tell the story of the first chapter of Job, using the carpet tiles method and cut outs of Job, his family and all his herds of animals. As each disaster strikes, the appropriate cut out is taken away until Job is left all on his own.

Talk together about how hard it is to stay cheerful when things keep going wrong, and how Job refused to let his suffering turn him away from God. Then help the children to make this model to help them remember.

Things to Sing

I'm black, I'm white, I'm short, I'm tall (WUW)
One more step along the world I go
Lord of the dance
Make me a channel of your peace

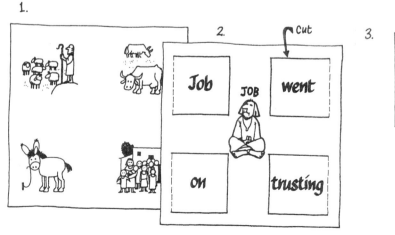

Join the two at the edges

Accepting God's Gift

Things to Read

Psalm 32
Isaiah 55
Galatians 3:1-14

Things to Do

Aim: Helping children to understand that we don't earn God's love, as it's freely given.

Have a nice box of chocolates on display as a prize. For the group to win it everyone must answer one question correctly. With the atmosphere of a quiz show, give each person a question they can definitely answer until the last person. (Make sure this is someone fairly self confident to avoid anyone being upset.) Ask this person a question which is impossible to answer, rather than just hard. For instance: Who is driving past West Leigh school at the moment?

Weather all the protests at the unfairness and impossibility of the question and savour the disappointment a little. Then explain that it's obvious they can't win the chocolates even though they all tried very hard, and that's the bad news. That's true with God's love as well – there's nothing we can do to earn it.

But there's good news, too. Jesus told us that God loves us all the time already. He offers us his love for free. (As you say this, take the wrapping off the chocolates ready to hand them round.) What we have to do is choose whether to say 'Yes please' or 'No thank you'. Go round the groups saying to each one, 'Will you enjoy one of my chocolates?' If they say 'Yes please' they can have one and you can all enjoy them together.

In a time of prayer remind them that God offers each of us his love to make our lives full of love and peace and joy. All we have to do is to say to him 'Yes please'.

Things to Sing

I'm black, I'm white, I'm short, I'm tall (WUW)
Jesus had all kinds of friends (WUW)
Give me oil in my lamp
Magic penny (CAP)
Love is his word (A)

TEMPTATION, SIN, FORGIVENESS

Resisting Temptation

Things to Read

Psalm 119:9-24
1 Samuel 26
Luke 22:1-23

Things to Sing

Jesus had all kinds of friends (WUW)
Out to the great wide world we go! (WUW)
It's me, O Lord (A)
Peace is flowing
Peace, perfect peace

Things to Do

Aim: To help the children to deal with temptation.

Have ready a sword and a mug of water, and introduce the story by looking at these two objects.

Tell the story of Saul and David, either acting it out or using moving figures on a floor story mat.

Talk about the very strong temptation most of us have to get our own back on someone who has been nasty to us. Think together about how David managed to resist the temptation to kill Saul. Link his love for God with his determination to honour and respect Saul.

Help the children make this sword and cup to remind them.

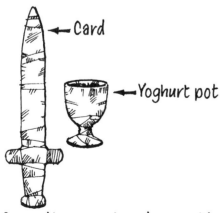

Cover the sword and cup with aluminium foil.

Strengthened by Hope

Things to Read

Psalm 147
Genesis 6:5-end

Things to Do

Aim: Sticking to what you know is right.

If you can bear the embarrassment, bring along a few things you have tried to make which have turned out badly, or something you loved which has got broken.

Begin by playing the 'sleeping lions' game, where everyone has to lie completely still however much the others tempt them to move. Talk together about how difficult it is to keep lying still when you are being encouraged to move, and how difficult it is to keep on doing what you know is right when everyone around is persuading you not to bother (e.g. not wanting to join in a 'be nasty to so-and-so' game; wanting to walk straight home from school when others want you to use a short-cut you've been told not to use).

Now, reveal to the children your disaster, or tell them about it. If any of them want to, they can share disasters they have had. Talk about how disappointed we feel when we try really hard to make something well and it turns out badly. Or how miserable we become when something we have made and are fond of gets broken.

That's how God felt and feels when he sees the people he has made so carefully all getting at one another and spoiling things. With the aid of pictures or models, get the children to help you tell the story of God rescuing Noah and the animals from the wicked world.

Help the children make this working model to remind them:

DON'T GET SUCKED IN – STICK TO WHAT'S RIGHT.

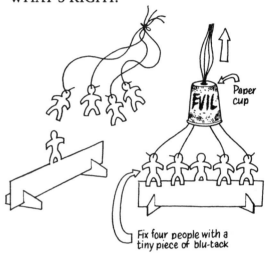

When you pull the strings, four people get tempted into evil, one stays where s/he is.

Things to Sing

All of the creatures God had made (WUW)
There's a rainbow in the sky (WUW)
God knows me (CAP)
It's me, O Lord (A)

Be Watchful

Things to Read

Isaiah 1:10-20
Luke 12:35-48

Things to Do

Aim: To help the children recognise that sin creeps up on us if we aren't watchful.

Give the children large labels to wear round their necks, or headbands which have on them such things as: being greedy, being mean, being unkind, being thoughtless, being rude, being lazy etc.

Play the 'Mr. Wolf' game with a difference, with all the evil creeping up on Mr. Wolf while he isn't looking. Mr. Wolf can only stop the evil getting at him by catching sight of someone moving. Point out that the more watchful he is the less chance there is of their getting him. Now read the passage from Luke 12 to them, and help them make a pair of cardboard binoculars to remind themselves to keep watchful.

Things to Sing

God made the earth (WUW)
Kum ba yah
It's me, O Lord (A)

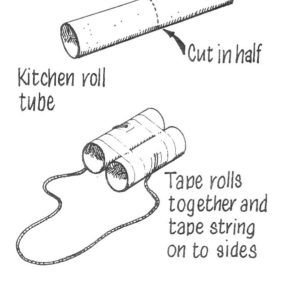

Cut in half

Kitchen roll tube

Tape rolls together and tape string on to sides

Go On – Admit It!

Things to Read

2 Samuel 12:1-23
Acts 9:1-22

Things to Do

Aim: for the children to see how God sorted out King David's sin and can sort ours out too.

Start by holding hands in small groups and getting into a real muddle. Then, still holding hands, try to straighten things out. We're going to think about how God sorts our lives out when we get in a muddle.

Explain simply and clearly what David had done – many of them will be familiar with such events through watching the soaps. Then read or tell Nathan's story. What do they think of the way the man behaved?

Tell them what David thought, and then how Nathan showed David that he was the man in the story. See if the children can work out why this was so, before going on to Nathan's words from God. Point out how David was forgiven as soon as he had said, 'I have sinned'. Whatever we do wrong, however badly we mess things up, God will always forgive us.

Then help them to make this card with instructions for what to do when we sin.

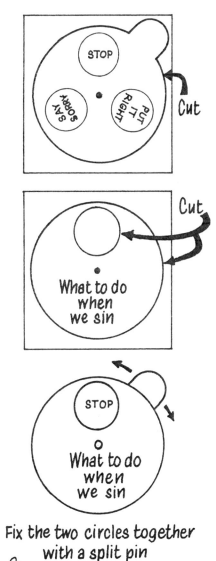

Fix the two circles together with a split pin

Things to Sing

Out to the great wide world we go! (WUW)
You shall go out with joy
It's me, O Lord (A)

53

'How Many Times Seven?'

Things to Read

Psalm 85
Psalm 133
Deuteronomy 30:1-10
Matthew 18:10-22

Things to Do

Aim: For the children to understand Jesus' teaching on forgiveness.

Take the disciples' question – 'How many times should we forgive someone when they have sinned against us?' Work out Jesus' answer as a sum, and explain that this means every time.

Ask if any of them can remember having to forgive someone for something. It is important that children are allowed to talk seriously about such things, because forgiving is hard whatever our age, especially if the wounding is deep. If we are not careful, and talk too glibly about forgiving, they may assume it's easy for adults and feel guilty for struggling and failing. They need their leaders to be quite frank about how difficult it can be, and how we sometimes have to keep working at it. They also need to know that we can all ask God to help us – giving us the grace we need to enable us to forgive others.

Look at the guidelines Jesus gave us about forgiving in the lost sheep story. Tell the story with some props or felt shapes on the story mat and make a note of what we have to do if we're good shepherds (e.g. wanting things to be put right, making the effort to go after them or make the first move in patching up a quarrel, being prepared to spend time on them, and being prepared to get a bit bruised and muddy).

Then, using card and cotton wool, each child can make a sheep to remind them.

Things to Sing

Jesus had all kinds of friends (WUW)
Out to the great wide world we go! (WUW)
Love is his word (A)

Stop Grumbling – Start Praying!

Things to Read

Psalm 119:9-24
Exodus 17:1-13

Things to Do

Aim: To familiarise the children with the Old Testament story of water from the rock.

Begin with any group of songs which involve a lot of dancing about and aerobic actions (such as 'I've got that joy' and 'Zip Bam Boo') so that everyone gets hot and thirsty. Have everyone sitting down and pour out some water for them all to drink, noticing how good it feels to drink water when you are really thirsty.

Now tell the story of the grumbling people of Israel in the desert and how Moses didn't grumble but went to God with the problem instead. That showed how much he trusted God, and God was able to help.

Talk together about the story and what it can teach us about talking to God about our worries instead of just getting angry and grumbling about things.

Help the children make the model of water coming out of the rock.

Things to Sing

He's got the whole world in his hand
The journey of life (CAP)
Water of life (CAP)

1. Cut out rock with slit in it

2. Thread six lengths of silver parcel string through the slit

3. Stick ends of thread at each end on to sticky tape

4. Pull strings to the back of the rock, so only the sticky tape is seen

5. Tap the rock, then pull on the sticky tape, and a stream of 'water' will gush out

WORSHIP, DISCIPLESHIP, MISSION

Yoked up to Jesus

Things to Read

Psalm 130
Psalm 49:1-5
Matthew 11:25-end

Things to Do

Aim: For the children to know that Jesus knows us by name and can really help us if we let him.

Start by providing strips of material or scarves for the children to try walking about three-legged with a partner. This doesn't have to be a competitive race – it's really the experience of learning to walk 'yoked up' to someone else that is important.

Now show the children some pictures from library history books of oxen yoked up together, and explain how the farmers would put a young, inexperienced animal yoked to a strong, experienced ox, so that the young one would learn how to work and the load wouldn't be so hard to pull. Talk together about their three-legged walks. They will probably have noticed how difficult it was at first with both pulling different ways, and how much easier it was once they had learnt to walk exactly in step with each other.

Now read the part from Matthew about Jesus' invitation to all the weary and heavily burdened. Why will it help to be yoked up with Jesus? Pray together for those who don't yet know that they can let Jesus take the strain in their lives and for all who carry burdens of some kind.

Then help the children to make this model of oxen yoked together.

OXEN Cut two out of thin card

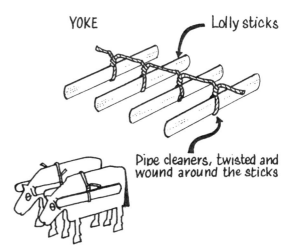

YOKE Lolly sticks

Pipe cleaners, twisted and wound around the sticks

Things to Sing

One more step along the world I go
Lord of the dance
Keep on travelling on (WUW)
Pick up your feet and go! (WUW)

The Real Thing

Things to Read

Psalm 121
Psalm 126
Acts 17:16-end

Things to Do

Aim: For the children to learn to accept God as he is.

Begin by playing 'monster consequences'. (Everyone draws a monster head, folds the paper down and passes it on. Now everyone draws a monster body, and so on.) Display the finished monsters and enjoy them.

There are also books available from libraries which have the pages split into three, and you can make your own combination pictures of an animal or person. You could use this kind of book, or make your own by drawing three pictures, cutting each into three and letting the children make them up into different pictures.

Explain how people invent gods, and tell them the story of Paul walking through Athens and noticing the altar to an unknown god, then using this as a starting point to tell them the good news of the one true God.

Then help the children to make their own 'photo-fit' kit. However they assemble it, the caption will always read the same: 'Our God never changes'.

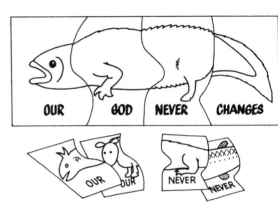

Things to Sing

Out to the great wide world we go! (WUW)
Come on and celebrate
Somebody greater (CAP)
Jubilate

Who's in Charge?

Things to Read

Psalm 63:1-9
Luke 16:19-end

Things to Do

Aim: To help the children learn to work with God at the helm of their lives.

First play 'traffic lights' where a caller shouts out either RED, AMBER or GREEN. If RED, they stop and sit down, if AMBER they crouch, and if GREEN they run about. Change the caller several times. Then talk about who was in charge during the game – was it the group leader, the ones who called out the colours or the children? (In a way it was all of these, because the group leader was in charge of the whole activity, the callers were in charge of what order to do things in and the children were in charge of themselves in keeping the rules.)

Now read or tell the story of Dives with the children helping you act it out. Dives was in charge of all his riches when he was alive; he thought he was in charge, anyway. Lazarus didn't feel in charge of anything. But they found out when they died that God was in charge. Dives wished and wished he had known that while he was still alive, because then he might have done things differently. Well, we *do* know that God is in charge, so we can make sure we spend time in God's company, then we'll know what he wants us to do with our lives. He won't push and shove; God hopes we will choose what is right, because he knows that will make us happy for ever, but he leaves us free to make our own choices between good and evil. Whichever we choose, God is still in charge.

Offer the children a choice of media to use to express the Dives story – perhaps crayons, paint or modelling clay.

Things to Sing

God is making a wonderful world (WUW)
I'm black, I'm white, I'm short, I'm tall (WUW)
I come like a beggar (CAP)
When I needed a neighbour

Be Prepared

Things to Read

Psalm 90
1 Timothy 6:6-end

Things to Do

Aim: To experience being prepared to do something.

Start by playing 'What's the secret?' You have a child at the front and give them items one by one. The other children have to guess what the child is being prepared for.

For instance, Jane might be given a leotard, some grease paint, a script, a ghastly costume and some ballet shoes. Her secret: she's going to be in a show.

Alexander is given a lunch pack, a torch, a rucksack, a pair of thick socks, a map and a pair of boots. (Nothing needs to fit, as the children won't be dressing up.) Alexander's secret: he's going on a night hike.

Sam is given a bag of flour and a bowl, some cheese and a grater, a tin of tomatoes, an onion and some oven gloves. His secret: he's going to make a pizza.

Now explain to the children how God prepares us in our lives and equips us for what he needs us to do. When Paul knew that his young friend Timothy was going to be a church worker, he wrote a letter full of advice. Read them a little of that letter so they can hear it as a personal one. Have another child in the front to be Timothy. This time we work backwards – we already know what he is being prepared for; we're going to work out what he might need for the job.

If you have a blackboard or flip chart you can write or draw what they suggest, which will probably be extremely practical!

Things to Sing

Out to the great wide world we go! (WUW)
Give me oil in my lamp
You shall go out with joy

Joseph and his Brothers

Things to Read

Psalm 119:73-80
Genesis 37:1-28
Luke 22:39-53

Things to Do

Aim: To teach the children the story of Joseph.

Tell the story of Joseph and his brothers, either with cut-out figures on the floor story mat or (if you don't mind anyone seeing your awful drawing!) draw quick sketches of the different parts of the story as you tell it. Simple figures like this are all you need.

Either draw on a long frieze or on different pages of a sketch book. Talk together about why the brothers hated Joseph, how Joseph might have felt as he was thrown down into the cistern, and when he was sold to the Ishmaelites. Look at how Reuben behaved differently from the rest of the brothers.

Now help them make this model of Joseph in his splendid coat.

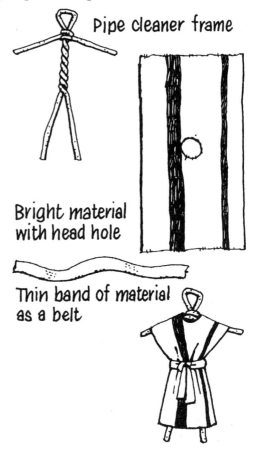

Pipe cleaner frame

Bright material with head hole

Thin band of material as a belt

Things to Sing

I'm black, I'm white, I'm short, I'm tall (WUW)
Out to the great wide world we go! (WUW)
Love is his word (A)
The family of man (CAP)

The Christian Challenge

Things to Read

Psalm 119:73-80
Amos 3:9-end
Matthew 26:31-56

Things to Do

Aim: To introduce the children to the challenging nature of being a Christian.

Begin by daring some volunteers to do various things, such as singing a nursery rhyme on their own, walking round the room blindfold, or putting their hands into a bowl of custard.

Ask how many who are at school may be laughed at or teased for coming to church. (This is very common in many areas.) Encourage these people by recognising that they have been daring to come here today. Anyone who is teased or insulted at home or school or work for being a Christian is being brave, and Jesus knows all about their courage.

Alternatively, play the 'What would you do?' game. Have a number of cards with situations on them. The children take turns in picking a card and saying what they would do in the circumstances. The others decide whether they think the person acted in the best way or not. No doubt you would like some ideas to start you off (before you think of any brilliant ones yourselves!), so here they are:

1. You are playing ball with some friends and the new ball rolls into the road. You don't want the ball to be squashed by a car. What do you do?

2. You keep finding the person who sits next to you is copying your work. What do you do?

3. Your swimming training is booked for a Sunday morning. There is no reason why it shouldn't be later in the day. What do you do?

4. Your group of friends is teasing you because you are being friendly to a child they don't like. What do you do?

Now tell them how Jesus made himself unpopular by pointing out ways in which the religious leaders were misunderstanding God's Law. The leaders didn't like the way Jesus was friends with bad people, either, and they thought he was being very rude to call God his Father. So although he hadn't done anything wrong, but had stood up for what was right, they came to arrest him in the night. We are followers of Jesus, and Jesus warns us that we won't always be very comfortable if we follow him. Do we dare to follow him?

Things to Sing

Out to the great wide world we go! (WUW)
When Jesus walked in Galilee (CAP)
Give me oil in my lamp
Put your hand in the hand (A)

Elisha and the Shunamite Boy

Things to Read

Psalm 139:1-18
2 Kings 4:8-37

Things to Do

Aim: To teach the story of Elisha healing the Shunamite boy.

Start with a game in pairs. The idea is that one of the pair tries to be a mirror image of the other – by really concentrating on the other person you start to reflect them.

That's like us with God; when friends of God stick really close to him they start to reflect him and begin to behave like him. Elisha was a very close friend of God so he was able to let God's love work through him to heal this boy.

Now tell the story with the children acting out the different parts as you direct them.

Together, make a cartoon strip of the story, with different children working on the main events:

1. The boy saying, 'My head, my head!'

2. The boy sitting on his Mum's lap.

3. Mum laying him on the bed.

4. Mum meeting Elisha and begging him to help.

5. Elisha breathing new life into the boy.

6. The boy sneezing and feeling better.

Collect the sections and photocopy them into booklets to give to the children next week.

Things to Sing

God is making a wonderful world (WUW)
God made the earth (WUW)
Out to the great wide world we go! (WUW)
I come like a beggar (CAP)
The best gift (CAP)

Trust in the Grace of God

Things to Read

Psalm 46
Isaiah 61
Ephesians 2:1-10

Things to Do

Aim: To see how God's glory is revealed in Jesus and in our lives.

You will need a beanbag, some pages from a magic painting book, brushes and water.

Begin in a circle (or several if the group is large), throwing a beanbag to everyone in turn. Practise throwing and catching in a way that challenges each person's skill – both hands, one hand, under one leg etc., and work at improving individual performance. Then stop using the beanbag, but pretend to carry on practising. Are we really getting anywhere now? No – we need the beanbag to practise beanbag skills! In the same way, we need God's grace to practise loving; if we don't ask for that or try to do the loving on our own, our Christian life will be just as empty as our pretending to catch and throw.

At this point have some prayer and a worship song such as 'Jesus, Jesus, can I tell you what I know' or 'I am a new creation'.

So when we do work in the grace of God, what happens? Give out the magic painting pages and watch the way all kinds of colours show up when we simply use water. In our lives, we will quite naturally show the colours of God's glory and the world will be a more caring, forgiving, happier place.

Things to Sing

God is making a wonderful world (WUW)
Out to the great wide world we go! (WUW)
This little light of mine (A)
Love is his word (A)
I come like a beggar (CAP)
When I needed a neighbour

Jesus Sends Us Out

Things to Read

Ezekiel 2:1-7
Matthew 10:1-22

Things to Do

Aim: To teach the children about the instructions Jesus gave when he sent the disciples out.

Prepare a few cards with instructions on them, such as: 'Walk round the circle and shake hands with everyone'; 'Walk to the table and find the biscuits, then offer one to the people wearing blue'; 'Hop round and offer a biscuit to everyone else'.

Now read or tell the children the story of Jesus sending his disciples out, counting up the number of disciples and writing each instruction on a board or flip chart. Talk together about why these instructions were given.

Make these drawstring purses with a prayer on the coins.

Things to Sing

Out to the great wide world we go! (WUW)
You shall go out with joy
Go, tell it on the mountain (CAP)
Jesus Christ is here (CAP)

LET YOUR WILL BE DONE

Hear the Word of God

Things to Read

Psalm 119:145-152
Jeremiah 36:9-end
Matthew 25:14-30

Things to Do

Aim: Learning to listen

First play this listening game. Tell the story from Jeremiah giving each person a part. Whenever they hear themselves mentioned, they stand up, turn around and sit down. At the mention of the fire, everyone moves. Afterwards, point out how they had all needed to listen to do that so well. Who in the story didn't want to hear what God had to say? Did he succeed in destroying God's word when he burnt the scrolls? (For a little while, but not for long.) Who was good at listening to God?

Now try listening to hear a pin drop, first with your ears blocked and then normally. Try looking at something with your eyes closed and then with them open. Try feeling something with thick gloves on and then without. That's how we are, sometimes; God communicates with us in lots of ways, but if we want to notice we'll have to listen carefully.

Help them make this pair of ears to remind themselves to listen to what God is saying.

Things to Sing

God made the earth (WUW)
Love is his word (A)
Kum ba yah
Peace, perfect peace (CAP)

Learning about God and Ourselves

Things to Read

Psalm 67
Deuteronomy 28:1-14
Matthew 6:5-13

Things to Do

Aim: For the children to become familiar with the Matthew passage and deepen their understanding of prayer.

Pin pictures or names of animals/people on the children's backs and set them off to find out who they are by asking other children questions about themselves. (No one is allowed to cheat by giving the answers away!) After a suitable time gather the children and ask each one what they think they are. Unpin them so they can see the full truth.

Talk about the way praying and reading the Bible help us to get to know what God is like and how we end up knowing more about ourselves as well. Read the way Jesus taught his friends to pray, and go through the Lord's Prayer simply and clearly so that they know what it means. Use whichever version is most helpful to children in your group.

Let the children draw around their hands and stick one section of the prayer on each finger so that they can use their fingers to help them pray. Try this out together, with spaces between the sections to give everyone time to think about what they are saying. Emphasise the truth that they are talking to someone who already knows them well and loves them very much.

1 Our Father in heaven
   hallowed be your name.
2 Let your kingdom come,
3 let your will be done
   on earth as it is in heaven.
4 Give us this day our daily bread
5 and forgive us our trespasses
6 as we forgive those who trespass
   against us.
7 And lead us not into temptation
8 but deliver us from evil.
9 For the kingdom, the power and the
   glory are yours
10 for ever and ever. Amen.

Things to Sing

Jesus had all kinds of friends (WUW)
Out to the great wide world we go! (WUW)
Love is his word (A)
You shall go out with joy
Kum ba yah

Blowing God's Trumpet

Things to Read

Psalm 93
Joshua 6:1-20

Things to Do

Aim: To help the children listen to God.

Begin by playing the 'keys' game, where everyone sits in a circle and one person sits blindfolded in the middle. Someone creeps round the outside of the circle, holding the keys, and the person in the middle has to listen to discover where they are. If they point directly to them, someone else can go in the middle.

Then have a time of quietness, listening to the sounds and praying through them.

Explain that Joshua, in today's story, listened to God and carried out his instructions, even though the instructions were very strange indeed.

Tell the story from a soldier's point of view, and have children standing up as the walls of Jericho so that when the army give their huge shout the walls can fall down.

Afterwards, help the children make trumpets (see below).

Things to Sing

Give me oil in my lamp
Jubilate
I've got that joy, joy, joy, joy
You shall go out with joy

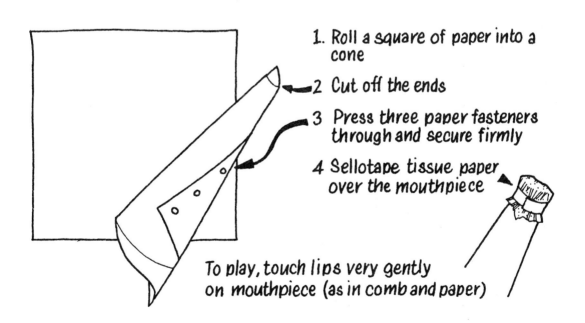

1. Roll a square of paper into a cone
2. Cut off the ends
3. Press three paper fasteners through and secure firmly
4. Sellotape tissue paper over the mouthpiece

To play, touch lips very gently on mouthpiece (as in comb and paper)

Family Matters

Things to Read

Psalm 103
Genesis 47:1-12

Things to Do

Aim: To see the settling of Jacob's family
in Egypt as part of the whole Bible story.

Have a timeline drawn on a long strip
of paper and on it fill in the main
characters and events of Genesis, as you
go on a whistle stop tour through to
Joseph and his brothers. The children
may be able to help you, filling in details
of individual stories as you go. When you
get to Joseph, slow the pace and increase
the detail, getting the children to join in
the acting out of the story, or using the
carpet tiles method of story telling. Make
sure the children are aware of the change
of place, and the region's geography.

Then make a communal model of the
whole family with their animals in
Goshen, using upturned bowls and plates
under a large cloth to make hills and
valleys, pipe cleaners and cloth for people
and paper cut-out sheep.

Things to Sing

I'm black, I'm white, I'm short, I'm tall
  (WUW)
The family of man (CAP)
When I needed a neighbour
One more step along the world I go

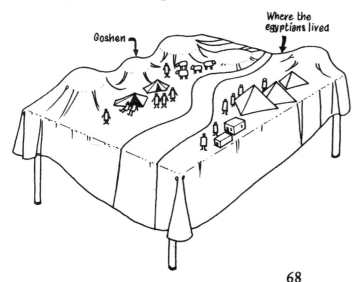

Goshen

Where the
egyptians lived

All in the Family

Things to Read

Psalm 103
Genesis 29:1-20

Things to Do

Aim: For the children to feel part of God's family.

Begin with the 'animal family' game. Everyone is told in a whisper what type of animal they are, and whether they are the Mum, Dad or Baby of that animal. Then everyone makes the animal noise, trying to meet up with the rest of the family. When they are ready, Dad stands behind a chair, Mum sits on the chair, and Baby sits on Mum's lap.

Now talk together about the things they like doing at home with their family – the people they live with. Write these up on a sheet of paper. Then talk about the things they don't enjoy and write these up on another sheet. It is important that the children accept that no home life is perfect; sometimes children think theirs is the only home where people shout at each other, and are relieved to find it's quite a normal part of family life for people to get cross with one another occasionally. In the discussion, talk about ways of making up and putting things right, and if any children don't want to contribute don't draw attention to them. Let the children pick something from each list to draw, and stick the pictures to the inside and outside of a paper plate. Round the rim on both sides write GOD'S LOVE . . . GOD'S LOVE . . . GOD'S LOVE . . . , so that they know that their own human family is held in the love of God, during both the good and the difficult times.

Paper plate

Things to Sing

I'm black, I'm white, I'm short, I'm tall (WUW)
Out to the great wide world we go (WUW)
The family of man (CAP)
The best gift (CAP)
God is love, his the care

Trouble with the Neighbours

Things to Read

Psalm 107:1-32
1 Kings 21
Matthew 7:1-12

Things to Do

Aim: To hear the 'bad neighbour' story and look at Jesus' teaching on how to live peaceably with others.

Begin by playing games of 'piggy in the middle', using beanbags. This is actually an excellent example of how the problem of being left out and then spoiling a game has been solved by its being made into a game.

Now tell the story of Naboth's vineyard. You could do this effectively by having it told from different viewpoints – first the king's, then the queen's, then Naboth's. Or you could have pictures of the main characters and, whenever they come into the story, display them on the floor or on an OHP. Or you could have children acting out the story as you narrate it, with everyone joining in the crowd scenes.

Whichever way you do it, bring out the underhand and cruel way Naboth was dealt with, and after the story talk with the children about what a bad and unjust thing it was to do. What do they think Ahab should have done? And suppose he had still become sulky, what do they think Jezebel should have done?

Now look at what Jesus said we should do – treat others as you would want them to treat you. See if they can learn this off by heart by singing it over and over again to the tune of 'Twinkle, twinkle, little star'. It fits in squashily, so long as you make 'treat others' fit with 'twinkle' like this:

| Twin-kle, | twin-kle, |
| Treat oth-ers as | you would-want |

| lit-tle | star |
| them to-treat | you |

It makes a tongue twister!

Things to Sing

God is making a wonderful world (WUW)
I'm black, I'm white, I'm short, I'm tall (WUW)
Out to the great wide world we go! (WUW)
When I needed a neighbour
Magic penny (A)

Be Good Neighbours

Things to Read

Luke 10:25-35
James 2:1-13

Things to Do

Aim: For the children to understand the teaching of James and to look at our own behaviour in the light of it.

First have a game where one end of the room is 'Being a good neighbour', the other end is 'Being a bad neighbour' and the middle is 'Names of people who are our neighbours'. As you call out something from the categories, everyone runs to the appropriate position. Good neighbour qualities may include such things as taking turns in a game, sometimes playing the game their friends want to play, helping at home without arguing, and making a get well card for someone in hospital. Bad neighbour qualities may include sulking if you don't get your own way, moaning about having to tidy your room, cheating at a game, and getting someone else into trouble when it's really your fault.

Names of neighbours may include the names of people in the parish (including some of the children's names), those they live with, share a table with at school, teachers they like and dislike, and friends and relations.

Then read or tell the story from Luke, using different voices for the various characters, and act out together the teaching in James so that they can see what ought to be done, as well.

Finally, help the children to make this circle of people joined in God's love,

which could be taken home to use as a table centrepiece.

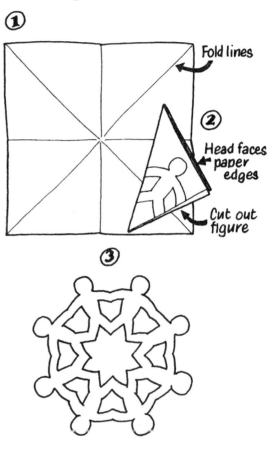

Things to Sing

I'm black, I'm white, I'm short, I'm tall (WUW)
Thank you, O God, for all our friends (WW)
When I needed a neighbour
The family of man (CAP)

Called to Serve

Things to Read

Psalm 123
Exodus 18:13-27
Acts 6:1-7

Things to Do

Aim: To think about how we can be a serving community.

Begin with an activity which can only work when everyone pulls together, such as parachute games or creating a structure out of bodies (as in some television advertisements). Then read or tell the events of Exodus 18, with the children acting it out. They can do all the queuing up for Moses and then make several queues once the other leaders have been chosen.

Using atlases and aid organisation materials to anchor the discussion in reality, talk together about how we can help people with their difficulties, such as housing, or not having fresh water.

Work together on creating posters for the event you plan to help.

Things to Sing

God is making a wonderful world (WUW)
Out to the great wide world we go! (WUW)
I come like a beggar (CAP)
The best gift (CAP)
When I needed a neighbour

Spread the Good News

Things to Read

Psalm 145:1-9
Acts 16:1-15

Things to Do

Aim: For the children to know the urgency of spreading the good news of God's love.

Beforehand, prepare some letters, cards and bills in envelopes, some of which bring bad, unwelcome news, while others bring good, encouraging news. Put them in a bag, and have one of the children as postman, delivering the post. As each item is delivered, it is opened up and read out. Everyone can make a suitable groan or thumbs up sign according to the news it brings.

Explain how some bad news is necessary, even if we don't like it, because it can help us put things right. Read or tell the events from Acts 16 where Paul, Timothy and Luke travel around wherever they feel God wants them to go, in order to bring people the good news of God's love which they know can fill their lives with colour and joy.

What kind of message would we like people to know about Jesus? Work on writing the messages, and illustrating them, before putting them in envelopes and sending them off to someone they know.

Things to Sing

Pick up your feet and go! (WUW)
Keep on travelling on! (WUW)
Out to the great wide world we go! (WUW)
Go, tell it on the mountain (CAP)
Jesus Christ is here (CAP)

The Good News Spread and Spread

Things to Read

Numbers 11:16-17,24-30
Acts 8:4-25

Things to Do

Aim: For them to get to know the story of Simon the Magus.

Get the children in a huddle in the centre of the room to tell them about how the early church met together and worshipped in Jerusalem. Explain that people started to persecute the Christians, especially the Greek speaking ones, so they scattered away from Jerusalem to be safe. (Some children are sent off in different directions.) One of these people was a man called Philip, and he went to Samaria.

How do you think God brought good out of these persecutions? All the Christians who were scattered went and told the people about Jesus wherever they went, so the good news spread and spread.

Now take everyone over to Samaria to watch what Philip was up to. Let the children act out the story as you tell them how Philip was gathering groups and telling them about God's love for them, healing the sick and giving the blind their sight in Jesus' name. Many believed, and Philip baptised them in the rivers. Among those being baptised was a person called Simon, who was a clever magician and was very impressed with what Philip was doing.

Now the Christians at Jerusalem sent Peter and John to find out what was going on. (Have two people coming over from Jerusalem.) They were very pleased to find all these new Christians in the land which was the home of the traditional Jews' enemy, and they laid hands on them so that they could receive the Holy Spirit. The new Christians started speaking in different tongues and dancing around full of the Spirit. Simon the magician wanted to buy this power so that he could do these things to people and have control over them. The apostles were furious that he should think such a thing, and had to pray over Simon for him to be freed from wanting power all the time. God's power is always freely given, and can never be bought, either by money or even by good deeds.

Help the children to express some part of this story in paints, crayons, collage or clay.

Things to Sing

I'm black, I'm white, I'm short, I'm tall (WUW)
Out to the great wide world we go! (WUW)
Go, tell it on the mountain (CAP)
Jesus Christ is here (CAP)

Build Your Life on Jesus

Things to Read

Proverbs 8:1-17
Luke 6:46-end

Things to Do

Aim: For the children to understand the sense of building their lives on Jesus.

Begin by talking about earthquakes and floods and have some pictures of what happens to houses that are built on a place where these things happen. Pray together for the people whose lives and property are destroyed or ruined in disasters like these. Why do people live in such dangerous areas? Usually because they can't live anywhere else. There's no way anyone would choose to build in an unsafe place. Then explain how Jesus said that anyone who hears God's word and, instead of following it, turns his back on it, is as barmy as this: someone actually choosing to build their house on sand, knowing that it won't survive the storms and floods.

Get the children to act out the story with their bodies becoming the houses and the floods and their voices the sound effects.

Give each child a small box to make into a house called 'Marion/Julian's life built on Jesus.' They can use the box at home to keep treasures in.

Things to Sing

Out to the great wide world we go! (WUW)
Give me oil in my lamp
Lord of the dance

No One is Left Out

Things to Read

Psalm 133
Ezekiel 37:15-end
Ephesians 2:11-end

Things to Do

Aim: For the children to understand the meaning of Jew, Gentile, Christian, and look at who can be what.

First talk about the different surnames in the groups, listing them as you do so, with all the different Christian names under the surname headings, so one family name may have several names listed.

Play a game where everyone is moving about until you call a family name. Only the members of that family carry on moving, the others must freeze.

Explain that we are members of that family because we were born or adopted into it, and that when we read about the Jews in the Bible it means people who were born as members of the Jewish race which could be traced right back to Abraham. No one else could be a Jew, and God chose this people to work through. Through them all the other nations of the world would eventually be saved.

Have two hoops labelled 'Jews' and 'Gentiles' and explain that the Jews were God's people of Israel and the Gentiles were everyone else. Have some names written on small cards, and ask the children to work out where they should go. Suggestions for names: Abraham, Goliath, Joseph, Moses, Pharaoh, Jesus, Mary, Peter, Paul, St. Francis and the names of the children.

Now take the hoops and names away and replace them with one hoop labelled 'Christian – a follower of Christ'. Scatter around the hoop these labels: men, women, boys, girls, people with black skin, people with pink skin, people who go to (West Leigh) school, people who support (an approved) football club, people who support (a rival) football club, Jews, Arabs, Indian people. Ask them to put into the hoop those they think can be Christians, and leave outside those who can't. (This may be interesting.) Draw them to the realisation that *everybody* can be a Christian, whether they are born as Jews or Gentiles. Now stick all the names in place inside a large circle painted on a sheet of paper and label the poster:
EVERYONE CAN BE A CHRISTIAN IF THEY CHOOSE – NO ONE IS LEFT OUT.

Things to Sing

I'm black, I'm white, I'm short, I'm tall (WUW)
Out to the great wide world we go! (WUW)
The family of man (CAP)
If I had a hammer (CAP)

The Story of Jonah

Things to Read

Psalm 119:41-56
Jonah 1-3

Things to Do

Aim: To look at some of God's surprising choices.

Start with a fast and furious game of choices. Label the corners of the room Tarshish, Nineveh, Home and Big Fish. The children take it in turn to shout out one of these words and then everyone races over to that place.

Then sit down and retell the Jonah story with their help. Whenever you mention:

Jonah, they say: What me, Lord?

Nineveh, they say: Disgusting!

Sailors, they get up and do four seconds of a hornpipe;

Big Fish, they open and close their mouths like fish;

and they make the appropriate noises when you say Wind and Sea.

Point out how Jonah was surprised and angry that God has chosen to save a place like Nineveh. We may be surprised at the jobs God chooses for us. He may need to use us at the shops, in the kitchen at home, down at the tip, in the middle of dinner or half way through a maths lesson.

Help the children to make this moving model of Jonah and the big fish.

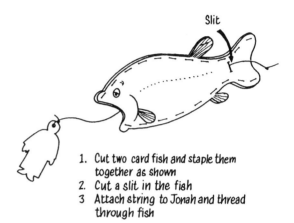

1. Cut two card fish and staple them together as shown
2. Cut a slit in the fish
3. Attach string to Jonah and thread through fish

Things to Sing

I'm black, I'm white, I'm short, I'm tall (WUW)
Out to the great wide world we go! (WUW)
Love is his word (A)
He's got the whole world in his hand
The family of man (CAP)

Keep Right On to the End

Things to Read

Psalm 108:1-5
Jeremiah 31:1-13
Philippians 2:1-11

Things to Do

Aim: For the children to learn how Jesus persevered right to the bitter end so as to win the victory over evil.

Begin by playing a game such as crab football or wastepaper basketball, in which one team is aiming to get through to the goal while the other team are trying to stop them.

Point out how games like this are like our life as Christians, when we are aiming to do what is God's will but it isn't always easy, and sometimes evil seems to be winning. Also, they may notice how the team members help one another, which is what happens to us – Christians help and encourage one another along the way.

Now read the passage from Philippians, and point out how Jesus was not going to give up however difficult or dangerous things became.

Help them to make this game to play at home to remind them.

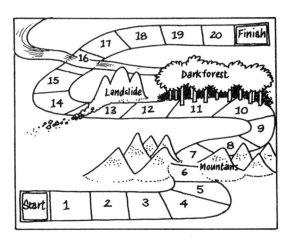

Things to Sing

He was born in the winter (WUW)
Keep on travelling on (WUW)
Jesus had all kinds of friends (WUW)
The journey of life (CAP)
One more step along the world I go

NEW LIFE IN CHRIST

Only God Gives Life

Things to Read

Exodus 32:1-7,15-24
Luke 7:11-17

Things to Do

Aim: To teach the children the stories of the golden calf and the widow of Nain.

Split the group into two and help each prepare a presentation of one of the stories. They can act, mime or work with puppets. Then let each group show their presentation to the other

Have a time to pray for the world – for anywhere they have seen on the news and want to pray for. It is helpful to have some pictures from the week's newspapers cut out and spread on the floor to help focus the prayer.

Things to Sing

Out to the great wide world we go! (WUW)
Go, tell it on the mountain (CAP)
Give me oil in my lamp
Jubilate

Real Death, Real Life

Things to Read

Psalm 66:1-9
Luke 23:26-49

Things to Do

Aim: To help the children understand how brokenness and dying are necessary for new life.

You will need some jam jars, blotting paper, beans and water, and a jar showing a bean which has already germinated.

Read to the children the story of the crucifixion from a children's Bible, *The Road to the Cross* (published by Kevin Mayhew) or use one of the children's video versions. (Think carefully about what you use, as it is important that you have something which is suitable for your particular age group and experience – some of the excellent adult film versions are very disturbing for young or sheltered children.)

All the violence and pain directed towards Jesus is difficult to cope with, and it may help the children to see how beans have to break apart to allow germination and new growth.

Arrange the beans in the jars like this, and keep the blotting paper very damp.

Damp blotting paper
Water

After the beans have germinated they can be transplanted into the garden.

Things to Sing

You can't pin Jesus down! (WUW)
Out to the great wide world we go! (WUW)
Lord of the dance
Jesus Christ is here (CAP)

New Life and New Hope

Things to Read

Genesis 8:15-9:17
1 Peter 3:18-end

Things to Do

Aim: For the children to see the connection between Noah's story and baptism.

Start with a game which directs attention to the different characteristics of water. When you call WATER! everyone 'flows' around the room. At ICE! everyone 'freezes', at RAIN! everyone jumps up and down on the spot, and at RAINBOW! everyone joins hands to make a semicircle.

Now tell the story of Noah, with children joining in with various sound effects and actions. Go through the actions and sounds with the children first, so they can listen out for where they come in the story.

Then show some pictures of baptisms, including some of total immersion. Explain how everything unloving, bad and selfish is being 'drowned' and the person being baptised is being reborn to a new, fresh life in Jesus. This is what Jesus taught us to do. Talk together about people they know who have been baptised recently, and if possible show the children the open font or baptistry and the things that are used in baptism.

Help the children to make a rainbow, (see below) which could perhaps be displayed in the baptistry area.

Things to Sing

There's a rainbow in the sky (WUW)
Rise and shine (A)
Make me a channel of your peace
Morning has broken

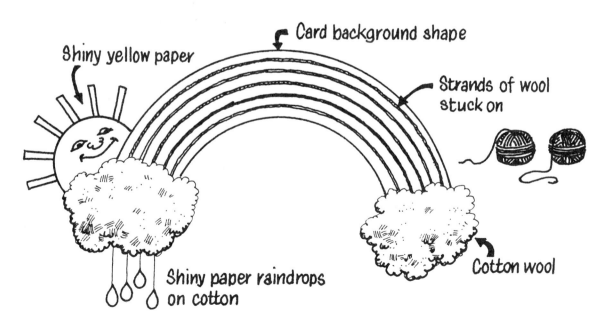

Card background shape

Shiny yellow paper

Strands of wool stuck on

Cotton wool

Shiny paper raindrops on cotton

Why Worry?

Things to Read

Psalm 19
2 Samuel 9
Matthew 6:24-end

Things to Do

Aim: For the children to understand the way seeking God and his righteousness can free their lives from worry and strain.

Have one child walking around the circle looking more and more worried as the other children call out things to make him worried (e.g. 'You're all on your own in the dark'; 'You've forgotten your swimming kit'; 'You're out shopping and suddenly realise everyone's gone home without you'). Talk with the children about the things that worry them. This may lead into a time of prayer, and may also provide leaders with insights which will help them to pray more specifically for the children during the week.

Now look at what Jesus has to say about worrying. Either read the passage from Matthew, or tell it in your own words with the children acting out dressing and eating and so on, so that you can then go through the reading again in actions, which will help them remember it.

Now split the children into small groups to go on a treasure hunt. Each team is given a coded clue to start them off, and when they have solved it they go to the leader who gives them the next clue to find something else. Eventually the clue words should make up the message:

STORE UP RICHES FOR YOURSELF
IN HEAVEN.

Things to Sing

I'm black, I'm white, I'm short, I'm tall (WUW)
Out to the great wide world we go! (WUW)
When Jesus walked in Galilee (CAP)
Peace, perfect peace (CAP)
Put your hand in the hand of the man from Galilee (CAP)

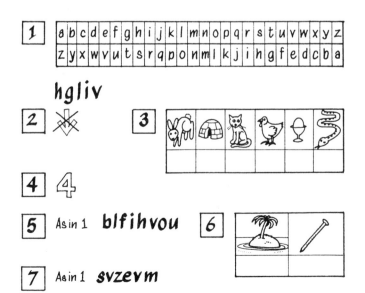

Real Wealth

Things to Read

Ecclesiastes 12:1-8
Luke 12:13-21

Things to Do

Aim: For the children to appreciate the lasting things and see the way other things don't last.

Start with blowing bubbles and enjoying them, noticing how we don't get terribly upset when they burst because we know that bubbles aren't built to last and we don't expect anything more from them. If we did, we'd get very disappointed every time one popped.

Explain how sometimes people set their hearts on things they think will last – like money and power. How long do these things last? Only to death, at the very most.

Now tell the story from Luke, introducing it as it is in the Bible – coming straight after two brothers wanting Jesus to sort out their squabble. (You may well have a couple of real squabbling brothers who would be happy to explain this part.).

During the telling of the story introduce some sound effects of the old barns being pulled down and the new ones built.

Either have these previously taped, or have them being made by the children.

Then help them to make this three dimensional picture which you can either look at or through, just as we can either fix our attention on this world and get disappointed, or we can look deeper into it and find real, lasting meaning.

1 Make a card frame

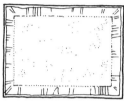

2 Stick coloured tissue paper on to the frame

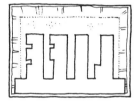

3 Cut out card shapes and stick on the back of frame

4 Look down at the picture and it is just a nice colour. Look up to the light and see LIFE

Things to Sing

God made the earth (WUW)
God is making a wonderful world (WUW)
Put your hand in the hand of the man from Galilee (CAP)
The best gift (CAP)

The God who Renews

Things to Read

Psalm 77
Isaiah 43:14-44:5
Mark 2:18-end

Things to Do

Aim: For the children to know that God doesn't just patch up, but makes new.

Take the children on a journey, using different parts of the building and/or churchyard, doing different sections of the story and teaching in different areas.

Begin in Egypt, and get them to tell you the familiar story of the people of Israel as slaves. When you get to the crossing of the sea, lead them out through two lines of chairs to the other side, where you can all rejoice that you are free. Lead them on to the Promised Land, where you tell them about how the people didn't stay faithful to God, but messed things up time after time until at last they were overcome and taken off to exile in Babylon. Move off to another area at this point. The people knew that although God had kept his promise they hadn't kept theirs and they knew they had messed things up. Now read excerpts from the prophet Isaiah to see what God said to his people and how he gave them hope. Then take the children on a whistle stop tour over the same journey, explaining it in terms of a person: we get stuck in a bad habit like being lazy or selfish or telling lies a lot, and God leads us out of it, but gradually we find we're messing things up again until our bad habits hold us again like exiles. So God's words of hope are for us, too; in Jesus we can be gradually made new. He will sort out and heal the things that make us behave badly.

Give the children balls of clay and let them model something good emerging from a shapeless lump. Display the models with a sign:
LOOK AT THE NEW THING I AM GOING TO DO. IT IS HAPPENING ALREADY – YOU CAN SEE IT NOW!

Things to Sing

God said: Folks we're going walkabout (WUW)
Keep on travelling on (WUW)
The journey of life (CAP)
One more step along the world I go
Give me oil in my lamp

Jesus Turns Life Inside Out

Things to Read

Micah 4:1-4
Matthew 5:43-end

Things to Sing

Out to the great wide world we go! (WUW)
Give me oil in my lamp
Lord of the dance
When I needed a neighbour

Things to Do

Aim: To look at how Jesus' teaching to love our enemies turns things inside out.

Show a quick clip of Tom and Jerry from a video, or some pictures from a comic strip. Why is Tom Jerry's enemy? How can they tell? Talk about other enemies they know about and/or have, and how that can be seen from the resulting behaviour.

Explain what the people of Jesus' time had been taught about how to treat their enemies (hate them).

Now read the passage from Matthew about loving our enemies as well as our friends, which really turns our normal behaviour inside out. Jesus doesn't say we mustn't have enemies; but he does tell us to love them if we have them!

Give the children these bags to make, which turn inside out to show God's way of living.

Plain material   Bright material

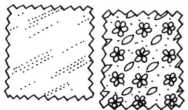  

A. Cut with pinking shears

B. Sew together with dull fabric on outside

C. Turn inside out to show bright fabric

Ascension

Things to Read

Luke 24:36-end
Revelation 5

Things to Do

Aim: To help the children understand why Jesus had to go away.

Show the children what looks like a blank sheet of paper but is in fact invisible writing. (You can use lemon juice for this or an invisible writing pen, widely available from toy shops.)

Explain that there is a hidden message on the paper, but they won't be able to receive the message unless something happens first.

Now make the message visible, either by using the other part of the invisible writing pen or by warming the sheet of paper with a hair drier if it is written in lemon juice. The word that emerges is POWER.

Go over the resurrection appearances and how the disciples saw Jesus going away from them so that he was no longer visible to them. We couldn't receive our message until something happened to the paper. The disciples couldn't receive

God's power – the power of his Spirit – unless Jesus left them in that particular time and place. Now he would be available to every person in every country in every age, including us!

Let them experiment with writing secret messages and making them visible again. Then give them a fresh sheet of paper on which they write in invisible ink: JESUS IS HERE. This is one for their family to discover at home.

Things to Sing

Out to the great wide world we go! (WUW)
I'm black, I'm white, I'm short, I'm tall (WUW)
Morning has broken
Give me oil in my lamp

Index of Uses

CHRISTIAN THEMES

THE CHURCH:
THE PEOPLE OF GOD

WORSHIP

THE CHURCH'S YEAR

INDEX OF BIBLICAL CHARACTERS

INDEX OF BIBLICAL REFERENCES